The

Courage

to be

True

Set Your Best Self Free

Tina Ruysseveldt

Published by Tina Ruysseveldt, September
ISBN: 978-1-7770727-0-4

Editor: Susan Crossman
Typeset: Luda Paul of Luda's Impressions
Portrait Photographer: Hudson Taylor

Life isn't **Easy**... this book is for **Everyone**!

ACKNOWLEDGEMENTS

I give thanks for my sobriety in the sure knowledge that, without it, I would have nothing. I also give special thanks to the program of Alcoholics Anonymous and the many members along the way who have courageously and generously shared their sacred stories, as well as their time and attention. Thank you to those who have both carried and supported me along the way.

I would like to take this special opportunity to recognize the value of not only the program of Alcoholics Anonymous, but also two of their publications. The book of Alcoholics Anonymous which sometimes is referred to as the "Big Book" and the Twelve Steps and Twelve Traditions, sometimes referred to as the "Twelve and Twelve". Both books have helped shape my ideas and thinking in sobriety and I am immensely grateful.

A special thank you to my oncologist, Dr. Andre Schuh, and the many nurses and health care professionals who kindly and compassionately cared for me at Trillium Health Partners, Mount Sinai and Princess Margaret Hospitals.

I was so lucky to be introduced to my final editor and typesetter, Garth Roberts and Luda Paul. Calgary sure came through for me. Garth and Luda were both professional and excellent at what they do, and a pleasure to work with. I appreciate you both. Thank you.

Thank you to my editor, Susan Crossman, for her professional advice and assistance in polishing this manuscript. Working with her made this scary, mountainous journey not only a reality, but enjoyable. I liked her the very first moment we connected and today I am proud to know her and consider her not only a colleague, but a friend. I cannot wait to read her up and coming memoir!

Thank you to my sweet Aunt Laurie for taking me in and being there for me when I had nobody else.

Thank you to my buddy Susie for always loving me where I was.

Thank you, Lynda, for being you, and for being there for me without judgment.

Gratitude and Love come to mind when I think of the Miles Nadal and Kelly Grier family. They brought me into their family and provided me with the love and support I needed to make it through all of the challenges and adversities that lay before me. Much love to you all. I will always cherish how each of you in your own way made me feel loved and allowed me to be part of your family. Thank you, Kelly, for walking alongside me. I know it was not always easy. I love you dearly and will never forget all you have been and are to me.

Thank you Kerri, my dear, sweet, wise, beautiful friend. Thank you for your unwavering love and presence and for making me feel like I was never alone.

Thanks to Patrick McCauley, who started out as my realtor and became my friend and angel. My gratitude to you for how often you gave me something to look forward to will never be forgotten.

Thank you to all of my friends, colleagues, and my yoga students who were there for me when I needed help. Whether it was a ride to the hospital, or the gift of some prepared food or sliced fruit, I thank you all.

As a recovering addict I have had a long journey in my ability to receive love and support and sometimes it was given and I was not able to acknowledge or receive it at the time. In particular I want to mention Veera Fernendes and anyone else that may feel overlooked or forgotten. I thank you from the bottom of my heart.

Thank you to my dear husband who not only has captured my heart, but takes such great care of it. Thank you for walking beside me and into my truth. You are truly an amazing partner and my best friend. We are "Better Together."

A NOTE TO THE READER

This book is my effort to humbly and openly share my living testimony of trials and tribulations with truth, honesty and raw candor. My wish is that you be able to identify your own story within my story and, in so doing, tap into the courage and truth that resides within you. I hope you'll feel inspired to take your own journey inward, safe in the knowledge that no matter how isolated you may feel, *You are not alone*. No matter how far off course you have gotten, there is a path out!

The stories I've shared in this book are intended to prompt open and honest conversations about the daily struggles we share in life. We all have them; we just don't talk about them very much.

Many of us today push ourselves too hard, and we rarely slow down. And it is becoming increasingly obvious that self-care should be our highest priority. It is possible for each one of us to improve our current quality of life by learning new coping strategies and by developing healthier lifestyle habits. This book represents my contribution to supporting you to do so.

May you trust that your instincts care about you and are working for your highest, best interests. May you know that you have the capacity within you to do the next right thing, and take appropriate actions to nourish and support your body, mind, and spirit. It's my wish this book act as a tool to inspire and instigate change so it may create a grand ripple of wellness through your life, and the lives of the people you care about. May you be on your way to set your best self free!

PREFACE

Thank you, Dr Stephanie Bot. I certainly never dreamt that I could or would ever write a book. I love numbers, math, and organic chemistry. Write a book? I don't think so. The truth is, I owe much of the credit for this achievement to my clinical psychologist, Dr. Stephanie Bot. Not only has my ongoing psychotherapy with her been a big part of my healing journey—and, in fact, I don't think this book would exist had she not encouraged me to do so.

At some point along my journey she said, "Your story is inspiring. It needs to be shared. It will help people." Even though I never set out to write a book, or bare my soul to the world (with a capital "V" for vulnerability), a seed was planted. The seed grew, and months later, in another session with Dr. Bot, I mentioned to her that I would like to share my story and that I needed a ghostwriter.

She asked me why I thought I needed a ghostwriter, and I said, "because I am not a writer and it would be easier." She replied, "But it's *your* story." There was a pause. And then I said "Okay." And I wrote the book.

Once I committed to the project, the amazing thing is the book took on a life of its own. My part was to make continued efforts towards its completion and along with the dedication required to do the work came the need to be continuously courageous. Telling one's own story is quite a daring and difficult experience and at times it wasn't easy. But it is in itself a healing process. Throughout the editing process—which took about a year—Dr Bot would once again prove to be invaluable. I have immense gratitude for her involvement in this book's inception and creation. I thank her for her caring brilliance and her belief, not only in me, but also in the importance of bringing important healing messages to the world.

CONTENTS

PROLOGUE

I lay on the floor of my living room in a puddle of vomit and wished with all my heart I were dead.

I'd been on another five-day bender and I'd been passed out for hours. The sleeping pills and sedatives I'd poured down my throat had come up with the rest of the contents of my stomach while I'd been lying in another drunken stupor. And I was pretty much just waiting for Death to claim me.

I'd been luring Death to my door for years by this point, shackled to The Drink I could not bear to be without, and this was not my first suicide attempt. Staying alive had become an impossible option and I had no inkling that it was even possible for me to live a life that wasn't completely dominated by my craving for alcohol.

I didn't consciously choose to burn my life to the ground in favor of "The Drink." I didn't suddenly one day decide to live a life of hard-partying so I could steer myself down a slippery slope leading towards the annihilation alcohol can so easily command.

The difficult truth that has taken me years to accept is I— and the people you know who are like me—didn't wake up one morning suddenly unable to control our alcohol consumption. Our problem isn't a lack of willpower. As hard as it may be for some people to hear, and as surprising as it is for many of us, the disease of alcoholism takes away our choice to drink.

I am an ICU Nurse, a Sexual Assault and Domestic Violence advanced practice Nurse, and a yoga instructor who created a therapy called Tina's Recovery Yoga ("TRY"). I am also a writer, a cancer survivor, a volunteer at the Centre for Addiction and Mental Health (CAMH), and a part-time student at the University of Toronto. But I sometimes introduce myself with the words, "Hi, my name is Tina and I am an alcoholic."

I have written this book to expand our world's understanding of the impact a dysfunctional childhood can have on us. It doesn't just help steer some of us towards a life of addiction; a traumatic childhood also sews the seeds for a life of unwellness on other fronts, as well. I've "been there and back" on a lot of different issues and I've worked hard over the past nine or so years to create a fulfilling life that I could never have previously imagined was possible for me.

This book represents my effort to take readers by the hand and share what I've learned about wellness and recovery. It's about how to free ourselves to be well. You might already be living a life that is fulfilling and empowering. But maybe it would serve you to free yourself from something that has been creating resistance—and therefore unhappiness—for you.

Do you need to free yourself from alcohol? Or from Secrets? Patterns of behaviour, perhaps? Or maybe you may need to free yourself from denial or the delusion you won't be affected by traumatic issues or events.

My own story started off pretty poorly and then it got worse, so you will read in these pages about some of the miseries related to what it's like to become an alcoholic, and what happens to us while we are in an active alcoholic phase of life. This book also shares some insights around the difficulties and latent gifts one receives while living with and through another demonized aspect of modern life: cancer. More than anything, though, my goal is to give people a glimpse into what life can be like after the drinking has ended, the cancer is in remission and years of healing are behind us ... how it's possible for life to keep shining on.

Believe it or not, there is hope. As humans, we have all struggled at some point or another with something. So, if you or someone you love is in a bad situation, or you find yourself stuck, in whatever way it may be, I want you to know that no matter how bad it may feel to you, you *can get through it*. When you read my story, I ask that you refrain from feeling sorry for me. I didn't write this book to evoke sympathy. I wrote this book to help others get through the unimaginable devastations that we sometimes encounter in life. I believe we each have our own journey—our own individual set of struggles—and I have a certain amount of trust that people will be able to read without judging either me or the people you know who have walked a similar path. If parts of this book make me seem self-centred, angry or victimized, I ask that you understand those are areas that still need work. Even today, I am a work in progress; I believe I always will be.

It is my wish that, after reading my story, the reader may begin to gain some insight into the cunning, baffling, and powerful disease of alcoholism. Falling prey to its power is about much more than a perceived lack of willpower. This disease is clever, deceptive and complicated. It talks to you, lies to you and tries to trip you up. It takes up residence in a part of your brain and resides there forever.

If you have an alcoholic in your life, or if you think you might be one yourself, I think it's important to understand the inner workings of this ferocious disease. And it's also important to understand how the allergy component of the Disease manifests in the physical body as an insurmountable craving that is enveloped by, and intertwined with, both a mental obsession and the physical need to drink. The obsession and craving are so strong that a woman with this disease is incapable of putting The Drink down, even though she promised to be at her daughter's dance recital later that day. She picks up another drink, knowing it won't be her last. The Drink trumps everything. It will push a person to the point where their "normal" becomes waking up after a night of drinking with the craving and need to drink that is so intense that they call into work "sick" again and again, knowing they will probably be fired for being absent so often. They have to pick up that next drink, maybe even before they are able to dial the phone. The need to drink is so powerful that once the allergy component of the Disease has been triggered in an alcoholic, they are rendered captive as soon as alcohol enters their bloodstream. The choice to drink or not drink is no longer their own. This is alcoholism, and this is my story.

So, what's it like to be an alcoholic? Picture, if you will, a set of cold, dark, damp, and rusty steps on a ladder leading down to a bed of red hot flames situated at the very bottom of a deep old well. Even though you know the flames are there at the bottom, and even though you know you will get burned, you still start down the stairway, going down deeper each day and moving closer to death each time you start the descent. That doesn't matter to you. You cannot stop drinking for anything, not for your children or even for your own life. This is what it felt like for me at the very end of my desperate drinking days. Upon awakening from yet another consecutive night of blackout drinking, I would cringe and tremble at the dark and desolate place my body and my soul had landed. I had begun to accept the harsh truth of my life and the reality of my situation. And I would put another drink to my lips and actually savour the taste and feel of the alcohol in my mouth. I was trapped, scared, and without hope. And I had no idea what to do about it. But I found a way to survive, not only the hold alcohol had on me, but also the vicious form of cancer that grew within me after I stopped drinking. When the unthinkable happens to us, it can be hard to find the way forward.

I dream of inspiring people to find their way and to find in themselves the tenacity, grit, and drive necessary to overcome their personal challenges or circumstances. My hope is that you will experience some resonating moments while reading this book, and make changes to do better and be better in your own life. As I started recovery, I created and implemented the LiveWell Recipe and, with its help, I was able to pull myself through a disastrous phase of my life and back into a manageable way of living. As time went on, it became clear to me my LiveWell Recipe was not just for alcoholics or cancer survivors, but for everyone, because hardship, is something that touches everyone's life. It is a tool to not only help us get through each day, but to uplift, improve, and help guide us to be well and LiveWell. It represents an all-inclusive recipe for people to make any amount of change in their lives that is necessary to simply live a better version of their existing life.

If this book is in your hands right now and you are reading, it is meant to be. May it bring you peace, hope, practical understanding and an abundance of light on the path ahead.

1

Setting the Stage for an Alcoholic Adulthood

My father stood belligerently over my mother and sneered at her as the tension between them grew. She was drunk again—and barely coherent—but she was nasty and mean and stumbling around the living room yelling at my father as I watched, scared and vigilant, from the kitchen. I hated it when my parents fought. But as a 12-year-old girl there was not a thing I could do about it. As far as I was concerned, at the time, mothers drank until they passed out and fathers yelled and stormed out of the house. Wasn't that what happened behind the closed doors of every house on the planet? My two brothers and I might not have been exactly happy about the scene playing out in front of us that night, but we had seen it before, and we would see it again. No big deal.

Except it was.

The argument between my parents escalated as I stood by, ready to step in and protect my mother if needed. I didn't know exactly how I was going to save her from my father's fury, but I knew she was at risk and I was filled with terror. I was ready to make my presence known. I would normally sit quietly in the stairwell nearby when my parents fought. In my family, it was always better to be out of the way than sitting in the line of fire. But this one particular night, I chose to stand in the kitchen where I could be seen, in hopes of providing some form of safety net for my mother. In my hopeful, innocent way, I thought I might serve as a referee, somehow.

My parents needed much more than a referee. As I watched, I witnessed my mother pick up a pair of scissors, hide them behind her back and then, in her drunken rage, lunge at my unsuspecting father and try to stab him in the chest. By the grace of God, he saw her coming, grabbed her arm and slugged her away. It was horrifying.

Stress, fear, and anxiety were woven into the fabric of my being from the moment of my birth. My baseline existence from early on—and as I grew up—was riddled with dysfunctional behaviour that did nothing to help my brothers and I feel safe and secure. There were times, of course, when an onlooker peeking at my family from outside the sturdy walls of our house might think everything appeared to be quite normal. But my world was full of uncertainty, fear, pain, and wonder, and it was punctuated by two questions: "Is this *really* normal?" And, "What's coming next?"

I grew up in the city of Brantford, a community that borders the Six Nations of the Grand River Indian Reserve in Southern Ontario. I was the middle child of three kids, and the only girl. My mother had become pregnant at 17 and by the time she was 22 she had three children under the age of five under her care; my older brother and I were born only 11 months and two weeks apart. The fact my parents were minimally educated didn't help the situation. My mother attended grade school only, and my father had obtained a Grade 12 education. The end result of all this was I started life with what sociologists call a very low socioeconomic status, which is not surprising. How could my young parents have possibly begun to provide for the needs of three young children? The instability in our household was made significantly worse by my mother's preoccupation with the bottle and my father's preoccupation with himself. The needs of both my parents took priority in our household, and it resulted in the opposite of anything that might be considered "child-centred care." Our need for love and support did not have a place in this family.

My mother's mother was an Indigenous person of Tuscarora descent, and she had lived on the Six Nations of the Grand River Indian Reservation as a girl. She attended a Residential School, called the Mohawk Institute, at the command of a Canadian Government that was focused on removing aboriginal children from their culture and traditions so they could be integrated and assimilated into the larger white Canadian culture. Much has been written about the residential schools' problem elsewhere, and we now know about the devastating impact it had on our Indigenous children. That impact still reverberates within the community today and it had a direct impact on my mother's experience as a child. My grandmother's traumatic experiences, in turn, meant my mother never received a solid maternal foundation upon which to pattern herself. So, it was no surprise my mother had skewed ideas and no model of how to parent and cope with the needs of her own children. This, coupled with her lack of resources, meant she had trouble caring for me and my two brothers in a way that provided the love and support we needed, and I know she wanted to give. She just hadn't been prepared for it.

When it came to my father's life, the truth is that my brothers and I had turned his world upside down. His youth had been stopped in its tracks and life as he knew it had drastically changed forever the day that first child made its way into his life. Things only got worse with every new baby that arrived. His life was different from what he had envisioned for himself and I could only imagine how it must have felt for him having had his youth taken away from him. Times were certainly different back then. My father had met my mother in the late 1960s and at that time, if you got a young girl pregnant you were held accountable for the results; the appropriate action was what was called a "shotgun wedding." And that is what my parents had. It was just what people did back then.

Memories of My Father

I can remember sitting in the back seat of my dad's black souped-up '69 Chevy when I was about seven years old as he chased the thrill of drag racing, one of his favourite pastimes. He had plunked me into the back seat, turned the key and when the engine roared to life, he pushed the accelerator to the floor, oblivious to the paralysis of terror that was afflicting my little body. My tiny hands held on for dear life to the seat in front of me, as my father defied his speedometer on a back road in the Brantford area. Imagine being afraid of roller coasters, but being forced into one anyway, and then having to sit, with your eyes closed and your hands locked in a death-grip onto the safety bar in front of you, until the cruel ride ends. My guess is my dad was trying to bring back that carefree childhood existence he had known earlier in life when he could just focus on what would bring him pleasure without the burden and worry of the family he had brought into the world. He was doing the best he could to get by and manage his young self in the life he was in. He had a strong work ethic and he worked on his car. And as many people in their early twenties do, he partied. I am not sure he knew how to fit parenting into this equation.

On my 10th birthday, my whole family went to the racetrack for the weekend to support my father while he raced his car. My birthday was on the Friday and that morning I woke up excited, as every kid is on their special day; I was anticipating a present. As it turned out, my parents had both forgotten it was my birthday, although when I reminded them they told me they would do something for me on the Sunday evening when we got home. That whole weekend centred around my father's racing as well as my mother's drinking and it was a painful time for me. When we got home on Sunday there was still no present or cake. My father had been advancing in the race competition and he had made it to the final round of the championship, which had been put over to the Monday because of a rain delay. I stayed behind at home alone that day. I was tired of being at the track and I had stopped hoping there would be some acknowledgment of my birthday. My mother went anyway, I'm assuming because the races allowed her to drink the way she wanted to, in a socially-acceptable environment, and that was her priority at the time. My father actually won that championship. He was so happy when he came home that Monday evening, and I was so sad.

Sunday Dinners

From the perspective of a mature adult who has seen enough of the world to know that there are many ways for families to conduct themselves, I realize now my parents absolutely did their best with the tools they had at their disposal. Both time and money felt scarce in our home and Sunday meals were not a normal part of our playbook. In fact, we very rarely ate together as a family, and there was no special fuss made over the idea of sitting down together and finding out how everyone's week had been. In my father's model of the world, there was no need for that kind of exchange. As an adult, I realized my father was limited emotionally and I do not fault him. He was not able to show accountability or responsibility for me or my siblings, nor did he provide for me in the way I feel a father should. He didn't understand what was needed to create the kind of loving and safe family that his children needed.

While I was in elementary school he provided a roof over my head and food in the fridge, but I needed something more than what he was able to provide. While I don't think he meant me any harm, I do believe his neglect inflicted a kind of injury on me. I desperately wanted to feel loved by him. I desperately wanted a meaningful relationship with him.

I don't think we felt very comfortable with each other, which would account for why he paid me very little attention. At the same time, I don't think this was a particularly personal thing, as it seemed to me that he saw most people as incidental entities, and he didn't seem to understand them as living breathing human beings who had needs. I didn't feel valued as a person, let alone a daughter, and my needs were, therefore, just not top of mind for him.

I remember shopping for a Father's Day card at a drug store with my brother when I was about 20 years old. One by one, we each picked up a card and read the message inside. The messages ranged from "Thank you for all the years of love and support," to "You have always been there for me." Each card made us laugh harder than the previous one because they were just so untrue. After reading four or five cards, we were literally falling on the floor laughing. This was in the late 1980s and there were no blank cards in those days, so we left without buying one. Not only did dad struggle to be a father, but my brother and I very nonchalantly accepted his poor showing in our lives. We had grown up regardless.

Later in life my dad sometimes figured out how to show up for me and for a time he would be there for me in ways a father would; I would get hopeful that this time things would be different. Even though from the outside looking in things may have looked normal, they weren't. I would refer to him as "dad," but I am not sure he really ever felt like one. Neither of us knew how to be or act in a healthy father-daughter way. At the same time, I didn't feel like I mattered much to my father and I wondered what might be wrong with me. What had I done wrong, and what should I do differently to merit my father's love?

Even while I was a cancer inpatient at Princess Margaret Hospital in Toronto, when my father was well into his sixties, I still found myself feeling a child's longing for a different kind of dad, one who would take care of me and take away the emotional pain of what I was experiencing. I wish he had known how to do that, but I imagine that his childhood hadn't equipped him well to be a loving father for me. I am now learning to forgive in a way that allows me to understand that a person's limitations prevent them from being the kind of person they might want to be. I have forgiven my dad, and in the sober adult part of my life, I have chosen to be a "fatherless." daughter. Today, I feel compassion for my dad.

I have learned that it's important to be grateful for what we receive, and less focused on what's missing. Being my dad's daughter was an interesting and painful path to navigate and

I wish now I could go back and give the little girl I was a hug, and tell her that she was beautiful, wonderful, and treasured.

My Mother Was an Alcoholic

My mother, meanwhile, was a horse of a different colour. Early on she worked as a seasonal labourer and a factory worker while managing the household and the care of her three young children, all with little-to-no help from my father. She was like many single working mothers who maintain households, care for children and hold down jobs. With incredible effort and hard work, women keep it together as they tap into the strong force within them. I like to think that my mother did her best but her alcoholism, and the personal demons she carried— combined with a baseline of poverty—left her struggling to properly provide care for us. From a very young age, my siblings and I often found ourselves alone and we had to try to take care of each other. As early as four years of age I have vague memories of waking up hungry and having an awareness that I was going to have to figure out how to get food for myself. This was our normal.

During the colder months, I often wished I could pull off a perfect trifecta of owning a hat, mitts and a scarf all at the same time, but proper winter clothing was a hit-or-miss kind of thing. I remember how special it felt to have my aunt braid my hair once because my own mom hardly ever fussed over me.

I remember habitually going to bed longing for love and attention; maybe for someone to take notice of me, to be interested in me. Wishing I could have the conventional good night kiss that seemed forever elusive in our family. I feel like the importance of what I am sharing is to know that we all have our own unique version of struggle in our upbringing. Some of you reading may have had your mom put out milk and cookies for you but you were left longing for her to sit with you. My point is that we were all left with longings.

As an adult, I have taken on the journey of self-discovery

as I was faced with a choice to either feel through my pain and live ... or continue to numb, drink and decline to who knows where. They say that you can't heal what you don't feel. I came to a point where I knew that if I didn't choose to feel, what happened would have continued to play out again and again in different venues in my life.

The sad truth was that my mother drank alcoholically off and on during our entire childhood. Alcoholic drinking is a term that applies to someone whose drinking generates negative consequences. People sometimes ask me how you know when someone really has a "drinking problem" and my first response is this: if drinking *causes* problems in your life, then it is a problem. For example, if you are fighting with your partner over too many late nights out drinking, then it is a problem. At the end of a workday, my mother would take the time to stop and pick up a bottle of wine at the liquor store, but she wouldn't stop at a grocery store to pick up milk for our cereal. Or she would spend as much time and energy necessary to schedule drinking into her life but she wouldn't go to events at school that were important or relevant to us kids. Her drinking was clearly a problem.

I can see how difficult it would have been for my mother to have been struggling with alcoholism as a young woman of 22 with three kids under the age of five. While sober, she managed to do some normal things for us, like cooking the occasional meal or driving us somewhere, but our home never benefited from the nice touches a devoted parent can bring— the occasional hot meal for breakfast, or time spent playing games together. I don't think I knew what to feel towards my mother when I was young because our home life was so chaotic. I loved her, yes, and she would often say that she loved me, but her words didn't always match her actions and this confused me.

My favorite memories of my mother date from when I was about 11 or 12 years old. During this time, she was "On the Wagon," a common phrase in the 1970s and 1980s, which meant simply to be refraining from drinking alcohol. I don't know how long she managed to stay away from booze, but it was long enough for her to receive her Registered Nursing Assistant certificate, which was referred to as an "RNA" designation.

It was at this time that I think my mom was happiest. There was less tension in our home because she was not drinking, and she was also earning an income. The house we lived in at the time had a small garden in the backyard and one beautiful sunny summer day my mom and I went into the backyard and picked radishes. We could smell the fresh lilacs that ran along the side of our house and after we washed the radishes we sat outside in the carport of our home and happily sprinkled salt on them, and ate them. I enjoyed that afternoon with my mother, and I felt happy.

I have another happy memory of waiting on the steps of the Brantford General Hospital for my mother to come off her shift so that I could walk home with her. The sad thing is that my mother would eventually be fired from that job at the Brantford Hospital after the bottle took over her life again.

As I grew up, my mother's drinking escalated and despite one or two fond memories, there is no getting away from the fact that I would always feel anxious when I drew close to my home. I never knew what level of tension I would meet upon crossing the threshold. Each time I turned the knob before walking through the door, I would be on guard and ready to quickly assess the version of my mom I would be faced with that day.

The Downward Spiral

As I look back now, I can see the downhill spiral of my mother's alcoholism and its ripple effect on the household. On some levels, we went through the downward spiral and whirlwind with her, as alcoholism is very much a family disease that affects everyone. I remember it became normal to come home for lunch to find mom passed out in a chair in the living room. I would smell her glass to see if it had booze in it and I learned to use this as the litmus test of what we were in for later in the day.

I remember the chocolate brown corduroy-like fabric of my mother's chair, the multi-coloured shag carpet, and the round, two-foot-tall ceramic table her drink sat on in the front room of our house. On one particular day, I could smell whiskey in mom's glass and it seemed a little strange to me. I knew mom didn't like or drink whiskey. Today I know she drank it that day because that's all there was in the house. When an alcoholic needs a drink, anything at all will do. Even with my disdain for the smell and taste of whiskey, I have been in the exact shoes my mother was in that day, and I, too, have drunk whiskey.

But as a little girl, I felt I needed to shelter my brothers from the truth about our mother. I told them our mom was just sleeping because she was tired, and I casually went about making our lunch. It was the 1970s and Chef Boyardee was popular … it was my favorite! But at age nine I was probably a little too young to be operating a stove on my own and no one had yet taught me how it was supposed to work.

I remember nervously and with great caution turning the burner on and anxiously waiting for our food to heat up. For me, it was just another step in life I had to figure out on my own. Later that evening, there was no sheltering my brothers from the yelling and screaming that ensued when my father came home and noticed how much my mom had been drinking. I think maybe, in that moment, I sensed, even though I was a child, that my mom wasn't going to be all right.

Over time I began to notice that if my mom was drinking, we were even more on our own than normal. What we needed from her would not be delivered and what I wanted her to be, she no longer could be. I learned to live with disappointment, and the pain associated with it, and at times I would internalize it all with the explanation that there was something wrong with me. To minimize the pain that I was feeling, I would act like I was okay, and pretend that everything was fine. On the inside, however, I was full of sadness and fear. Even so, I held strongly onto the hope and faith that everything would be okay, and that things in my world would be better the next day ... or someday.

I became adept at sizing things up quickly because when my mother had alcohol in her system, she was different. I didn't like it, and I didn't like her. Sometimes there would be only subtle changes in her behaviour, like a slight change in her voice, or maybe just a vague sense that she was somehow a slightly different person. Other times, when she had been drinking heavily, I couldn't stand to be in the room with her. Due to the progression of the Disease, my mother would sometimes change from reasonable "Dr. Jekyll" to hideous "Mrs. Hyde." When this happened, it would be extremely uncomfortable and scary to be around her, as the alcohol would render her capable of doing absurd and shocking things, and she would often become destructive and aggressive. She would become a blamer, and often her anger would be directed towards my father. It was hard for me to find a way to like her when she behaved that way.

Finding Relief Behind Closed Doors

When my mother was in this "Mrs. Hyde" state while we were at home behind closed doors, I would feel frightened and scared, and not sure if I should hide out in my room, or be near my mom just in case she might need me. This state change happened occasionally when we were out in public and it was embarrassing, as my mother would become loud and boisterous, and she would make little sense. I can still remember feeling embarrassed and sad at the same time—for both of us—when my mother and I went somewhere on the city bus one day. I wanted to hide to get away from the onlookers whose eyes were full of pity as they looked at us. It was a relief to finally get back behind closed doors at home, where all I had to do was feel scared, and where the embarrassment would be gone. I had a lot of inner conflicts because my feelings about my mother were complicated, tangled, and scattered. I always wanted something more from her but, at the same time, I couldn't understand why I didn't actually like her. I felt bad about it, as though there were something wrong with me because of how I felt. I mean, what kid doesn't like their mother?! The truth is, I never liked my mother when she was drinking, and the full circle fact is that when I grew up and alcohol began to take me over, I never liked myself, either.

It seemed that my father didn't like my mother when she was drinking any more than I did, and the number of fights in our household increased with every passing year. Looking back now, having known the experience of being an alcoholic myself, I can see that there came a point when my mother's drinking had spiraled out of her control. She was no longer in the driver's seat and she had crossed the invisible line of no return that differentiates a heavy drinker from an alcoholic. This is the point where the individual loses power over The Drink and their life begins to become unmanageable. To be drunk at lunch when your kids come home is a sign that you have crossed the invisible line. To get smashed at a public function is a sign that you have crossed the invisible line. To get black-out drunk and then wake up naked with a stranger means you have crossed that invisible line. A person experiences a blackout when they simply cannot remember where they were, who they were with, or what they did. It is a time frame with complete amnesia and there is no conscious override possible for one's behaviour. And it happens once you're on the other side of that invisible line. I witnessed my mother struggle as she sank further and deeper into her alcoholism, not knowing at the time that I, too, would struggle and become familiar with the very same demon that would ultimately drag me over that very same line. This is the point where a person can no longer drink without consequence or disaster. It's a point of irreversibility, where one's ability to control one's alcohol intake disappears, and there is now no way of ever turning back to normal drinking. Somewhere in the crossing of this line is also what I believe is tangible proof that one has indeed turned into an alcoholic and there is no going back, just like there is no way of turning a pickle back into a cucumber. Once this line is crossed, there is no way to ever drink safely again. It is a terrifying, life-changing state to accede to, and one that I believe most alcoholics experience in silence. I did, partly because I knew that if I said anything about what was happening to me aloud to another person, I was more or less admitting that I was an alcoholic, which I was not ready to do. My silence also stemmed partly from the fact that I simply didn't know where to turn.

For an alcoholic, the terrifying, heavyweight of the truth becomes apparent as we begin to see that we are no longer in control of The Drink; we are in its grip. The realization of our powerlessness settles in. This is a very difficult concept to grasp and it's extremely difficult to understand unless you, yourself, are experiencing it. But I will do my best. Please keep in mind that this is a written account of my experiences and the opinions I have formulated as a result of both being an alcoholic and growing up in an alcoholic home.

My mother continued drinking throughout the rest of her life, and the effects of her drinking ravaged her existence. The Drink took her through treatment centres, detoxes, suicide attempts, loss of employment, fractured relationships, and a life filled with anger and resentment. The pain, turmoil, and tragedies of alcoholism marred my mother's life, and she died a sad alcoholic death at age 60. The Drink ruled each day of her life right up until her death. Despite all that, my mother showed incredible determination, tenacity and grit. She once told me that she wasn't able to attend high school because she had to enter the workforce and help out at home. Against the odds, while in her thirties and still drinking whenever she could, she successfully completed her General Educational

Development (GED) accreditation and went on to be accepted into the Nursing Program at George Brown College in Toronto, Ontario. How she managed, I don't know. I do know that something happened during her clinical period and she actually thought about quitting the program. I have a sense it had to do with drinking, but ultimately one of her teachers called her at home and talked her into not giving up. When they talk of teachers changing lives, well, this one did. I wish I knew this teacher's name so I could personally thank her.

My mother graduated and she was an amazing nurse— she actually won the Nursing Bedside Award in 1978 when she graduated as a Registered Nursing Assistant. So now here she was a Registered Nurse in 1990 with a dream to head down south and work in Texas. During those times, there was a reciprocity arrangement between Canada and the United States and in particular one with the state of Texas. To be eligible to obtain a "TN work Visa," as it was called, a student was required to have achieved a score of > 350 on the College of Nurses of Ontario Exam. I was with my mom on the day she received the envelope in the mail. She was so nervous and excited that she couldn't bear to open it, so she handed it right over to me. I ripped that envelope open, and there it was, she had done it. She had scored 372 ... and off to Texas she went. But, sadly, her drinking was doomed to affect her professional life. I was witness to this happening while visiting her in Texas. She drank a lot the first night of my visit and the next day she did get up and go to work, but she was sent home for being under the influence of alcohol and it was horrible. I am not sure if she had actually succumbed to the craving and The Drink that morning and actually had taken a drink before going to work, or if it was the residual of the amount of alcohol she had consumed the previous night. Nonetheless, she was sent home for smelling of alcohol. She was able to keep her job by agreeing to random urine alcohol screening tests. I remember being with my mother when she received a call requesting she be tested and we went immediately to a lab so she could complete the testing within the required time frame.

I can only imagine the level of stress my mother was under in those years. Every waking moment was a wrestling match for her as she dealt with both her fear of drinking again and the risks involved, and her intense craving and need to drink. The stress was so intense that she attempted suicide shortly after my visit. My brother and I flew down immediately and spent a weekend visiting her at the psychiatric hospital. While there we emptied her apartment of alcohol and went back to our lives in Canada. It was all we could think of to do. What my mother did next actually saved her nursing career. She went to unusual and great lengths to try to manage her drinking by moving to Saudi Arabia, where alcohol is completely banned. There she could more safely live and work as a nurse because she could distance herself from her Disease. It helped her stay sober and she lived and worked sober and proud there for many years. I am so proud of my mother to be the first person in her family to ever graduate from college. She overcame a lot to create these achievements, and I have her to thank for where I am today. I am my mother's daughter.

The Question to Ask Yourself:

Do I have an unhealthy behavior that is not allowing me to be my best?

2

How Not to Parent

I was crouched down on the shag carpet in front of the Christmas tree wearing a flannel nighty that my grandma had sewn for me one year when someone snapped a picture of me. In the picture I had my knees tucked tightly into my little body and I was clinging to a small doll; I was almost smiling. I don't think I could have actually smiled if I tried because there was not much to smile about in my world. If you peeled one layer off that photo you would be able to see how fearful I was, how frightened and confused.

But there were compensations. Since our parents were wrapped up in their own journeys it was natural that my older brother and I learned to be each other's support system; we became each other's lifeline. Pictures taken of us as young children usually show the two of us together, his arms wrapped around me, holding me close, as if to protect me. We had nowhere else to go so we looked to each other for much of the love and support that our parents failed to give us. We became the only consistent variable in each other's lives. I felt protected and safe whenever my older brother was near. By the time I was about five years old, my father had started to connect quite strongly with my younger brother, but this left both my older brother and I feeling more cast to the side than ever. My father parented according to quite a simple pattern: he paid my older brother angry attention, he paid me no attention, and he gave my younger brother devoted attention. I will never understand this, but I am sure in the world of psychology there is an explanation that is sensible, based on the circumstances we all faced. The situation meant my older brother and I felt alone and pitted against the world. My mother continued to drink alcoholically, which rendered her unavailable to us most of the time.

My brother was my rock. We were there for each other and we trusted and depended on each other. That being said, the relationship I had with my brother had no emotional boundaries, and it did have aspects of emotional incest to it. It worked for both of us for many years—up until we were in our early twenties—but it got in the way when we started finding partners of our own.

We didn't know how to be present with each other while maintaining romantic relationships with other people. I included my brother in couples' activities more often than I should have, and it appeared that the only way he could manage our relationship was to keep me at a contained distance when he was seeing someone else. This was terribly painful for me when it happened. Now, years later, and after much therapy, I understand the dynamics behind our relationship so that it no longer pains me. But at the time, it was tough.

Making Hash Brownies

As my childhood years played out my parents partied a lot in the house, especially on weekends, and they drank and did drugs fairly openly in front of us. On one occasion in the 1970s they had invited some friends over and they decided to make some hash brownies. At the time, processed food was the latest and greatest thing and the processed brownie box of choice was something called Snackin' Cake, which I loved. It was difficult to grasp at age 10 that I could not have a piece of the chocolate cake that I smelled baking in the oven. And I became used to how parenting in those days was typically delivered in the form of four words, delivered by my father: "Get in the Basement." And we did: my brothers and I just kept out of our parents' way.

My dad made us feel like we were lucky to be allowed to live under his roof and it was almost as though we owed him something. I often felt as though I was a burden, and, right or wrong, my father's attitude towards me often had me wondering if I would ever be a wanted child, although I am sure that was not his intention.

In fact, I'm sure that no person would set out to parent that way. Neither of my parents were equipped for the task in front of them, and they didn't know how to do things any differently. I have very few memories of feeling comfortable in my home and I now recognize that I experienced what many psychologists consider an emotionally and materially impoverished childhood.

Like many other children in a similar situation, I lived in a constant state of insecurity and uncertainty and I always felt in need of something that was lacking: a meal, some affection, or a sense of belonging. To survive this kind of neglect, I would tell myself that I was fine and I would push feelings of exclusion and loneliness away. I would act like a normal, happy child. I never let my true feelings show, even though I was dying on the inside, wanting and wishing for something *more*.

I learned to accept that I had to expect nothing, make do, and improvise. We had no choice but to accept the home we were given as normal, and to survive. My mom and dad floundered as they played out their roles in the grown-up game of parenting. They both struggled, which is not surprising, as they were still growing up themselves, and they never had the time to figure out how to navigate their own needs, let alone look after ours. This was a drama that played out at our expense, as the needs of our parents were always their first and sometimes only priority; they were incapable of meeting ours.

The gift of incredible determination, tenacity, and grit that I believe I inherited from my mother proved to be a life-altering quality that by the grace of God I could access when pressed. At the time, I really didn't know what this quality was all about, but as I got older I began to call it my Inner Spirit Drive and I came to believe that it gave me the resources I needed to deal with what was going on around me. The very same energy that was propelling me forward would also protect me in times of great need later on in my journey. Looking back, I can see that there were moments of light always shining through.

In my early years, my mother showed up some of the time, but by age 11 or so, I started assuming that she, too, would let me down. I became the kid in the class whose parents never put in an appearance. At the time I thought that, if I acted as though everything were okay, things just wouldn't be so bad. But on some level, I knew things were not right and I also knew enough to cover it up. Once, when I was 10 years old and in Grade 5, my teacher, Mrs. Boyce, asked me if everything was all right at home. I don't remember what I said to her but I do remember I wasn't truthful, I knew what I had to say to protect my parents.

My parents missed dance recitals, ball games, track and field events, graduations, and, as I mentioned earlier, sometimes even birthdays. For a long time, it seemed normal for the parents in a family to be unreliable but eventually, I realized that other parents attended their children's milestone events. It became very hurtful to be the unattended kid and I continued to make excuses for my parents. At the same time, I thought that maybe, if I deserved my parents' attention, they would give it.

Missing in Action

The evening of my Grade 8 dance recital brought this feeling of unworthiness directly home to my heart.

It was my final year of dance classes and I was extra-excited that I was finally old enough to do the top-hat-and-cane dance.

Although this was an opportunity for my parents to see me shine on stage, they failed to show up. I scanned the audience for their faces during each of the five numbers I performed and I left the stage every time feeling an ache inside when I realized my parents were still not in the audience.

As the evening wore on it became increasingly difficult to get out on stage and perform. But I did, and I acted like it was okay. But it wasn't.

Nor did my parents feel motivated to attend my Grade 8 graduation, and this time the other parents noticed that they were absent. I still remember my dress, and I remember the shame and embarrassment I felt while the other parents looked at me.

I caught snippets of their quiet conversations as they talked about the fact that I was alone. I tried to stand as tall as I could but I ached inside. And I felt less worthy than ever. There must be something really wrong with a kid whose parents refused to attend their graduation ceremony, I thought. This had to be my fault somehow. All the other parents were there, why didn't mine come? I did end up going out for pizza that night, as some kind parents took me under their wing and took me along for the celebration. It was nice to eat pizza and not be hungry, but it was not a pleasant evening for me.

Until recently I had trouble acknowledging the gravity of the neglect both my parents inflicted on us kids.

For years I had been much more forgiving of my mother, perhaps because I share this disease with her. Or maybe it was a mother-daughter thing. It took me a long time to see that she was really no better than my father.

I think part of what pained me the most about my parents' neglect was that I took it to mean that I wasn't wanted or loved. In my child's mind way of thinking, I measured their love for me by the amount of time they spent with me. My mother loved the bottle and my father loved his race car. Right or wrong, it seems that at times I was nothing more than collateral damage.

Questions to Ask Yourself:
Do I carry anger towards my parents or my caregivers? Can I look at them with compassion so that I may free myself from this unhealthy energy?

3

Sex and Self-Esteem

One of the fallouts of having parents that didn't give me the hand I needed in my upbringing was that I was not taught to respect and honor my body. I came of age during the 1970s when there was very little sex education available, and certainly "relationship management" was not taught in school. By this time my mother was in no shape to have life discussions with me, nor were her insights likely to be valuable. I learned from what I saw around me and from what happened to me.

In fairness to my father, living with an alcoholic is not easy, but I did witness my mother endure physical abuse at the hands of my father. I will say nothing about him regarding this matter except that he was neither strong enough nor psychologically equipped to handle the situations my mother's alcoholic episodes required of him. My mother's inappropriate behaviour—which was sometimes aggressive in nature—elicited an aggressive response from my father that seemed appropriate to me. Often he did nothing more than yell or argue loudly, or maybe he would give her just a smack or two. But sometimes things would escalate. Sometimes this terrified me.

One day I noticed my mother had a small chunk missing out of her ear lobe. It had started to scab over and it looked very painful to me. Even today I can still conjure up an image of the wound. I came to learn that my parents had been driving on the highway the previous day and my mother had been drunk and in what I now believe to be a blackout state. Out of the blue she reached over and slammed the gearshift into reverse. After regaining control of the vehicle my father had slugged her hard enough to inflict the wound.

I had often wondered what had happened in my mother's

younger life to perpetuate her slide into alcoholism and add to the pain she carried. Ultimately I did learn that a man living in her childhood home had sexually abused her and that she had not been heard when she had spoken up. I am sure that it was difficult for her to carry, as it is for anyone in that situation. I am hopeful for women as we move forward, especially because in recent years, the #MeToo Movement has brought much-needed awareness, conversation and support to women who find the courage to come forward and speak up, as my mother tried to do.

Uncomfortable and Confused

Like many other women of my generation, the sexual messages I picked up during my adolescent years in the 1970s and 1980s left me feeling uncomfortable and confused. Despite the efforts of "Women's Libbers" at the time, women were commonly looked at as sex objects and there was not much to be done about the matter. I am sure many of you remember when "catcalling" was common and pretty much acceptable. I remember how uncomfortable it was to walk by construction sites in my youth, so much so that today when I walk by one, I am relieved when I hear no whistles or jeers. I am grateful that this behaviour has faded into history enough that young women growing up today are not subjected to it as much.

My first sexual experience happened when I was 12 years old and it validated this insidious cultural belief that women had value primarily as sex objects. On this particular day, one of my brothers took me to his best friend's house and once we were there he told me to go with his friend into the tent that had been set up in the back yard. I do not remember exactly what my brother said, but I trusted him implicitly and so I went with his friend. At the same time, I felt scared and uncomfortable. On some level, I knew that there was something wrong with the situation. But I went into the tent and I did what the friend asked. Meanwhile, my brother went with another girl into the house. It is disturbing to me now that the two boys had prearranged sexual experiences for each other by each bringing a girl for the other's use. And at the same time, I didn't have to comply. No aggression or violence was required to get me to cross the bridge into sexual behaviour designed solely for a male's pleasure. But I think now that there were a number of reasons why I went along with the plan. First of all, my brother was a beacon of safety in a chaotic world. I trusted him. At the same time, I was culturally programmed to accept this kind of behaviour as a normal part of male-female relations. I was seeing women being treated as sex objects all the time on TV and in magazine ads. My own mother appeared to exist for my father's convenience and he didn't seem to respect her very much. Was this normal for male-female relationships? But, more to the point, my self-esteem had been so obliterated by a life of doing without that it didn't occur to me that there actually might be a choice here. While this was all happening, I remember feeling confused. I was afraid to say no, but the entire episode reinforced the lesson I had already learned in life, that what I wanted was so unimportant that it was pointless to object. So I didn't.

I don't remember many details of that particular incident, or of the afternoon itself, although I do remember the events leading up to the moment I entered the tent. I don't think the boy was able to complete his intended task, but my memory is somewhat vague in that detail. It was almost as though I were having an out-of-body experience—and I felt unsure, scared, confused, and ashamed. I don't remember leaving to go home that day, but I vaguely remember acting like everything was okay. The truth was that I was not okay, and very little else in my world was okay, either. I still remember the name of my brother's friend, and I remember the location of his house, and what the house itself looked like. Harm was done that day, harm that would linger. This experience became a burdensome secret that changed me and affected me deeply. Each of us who was present that day has had to carry this secret. As much as human beings like to think that our individual makeup is different from our fellows, none of us is exempt from the carcinogenic effects of secrets.

This reminds me of a phrase I read in Theo Fleury's book *Playing with Fire*.[1] As Theo shares in his book, he was sexually abused as a young boy by his hockey coach and he kept the incident secret for many years. As an adult, while he himself was attending Alcoholics Anonymous (AA) meetings and trying to get sober, he heard someone say, "You're only as sick as your secrets." When I first read this phrase in Theo Fleury's book, it resonated down into the depths of my soul. I thought, "Whoa … that's not good," and then my next thought was, "I'm screwed." I was gripped with fear because the truth was that I had countless secrets, some of which I didn't even consider to be secrets, I had just categorized them as things I didn't tell people, maybe in the hopes that they wouldn't exist if I didn't say them out loud. The problem was that they did exist and they were real. Each secret we have is embedded in the fabric of our being, hidden away yet carried, day in and day out. I knew in that moment that I had to unleash my secrets if I wanted to survive. I had to work through them and set them free. I believe this to be a very powerful truth. Thank you, Theo.

Instincts in Collision

The AA Big Book says that harm results when instincts are in collision. This happens because each person is trying to get their own needs met without carefully considering the needs of others. I think this is what happened the day my brother served me to his friend for sex. I don't think my brother intentionally meant me any harm, but while he was pursuing what he wanted for pleasure, he was not respecting me or thinking of my needs at all. And I imagine that some of you reading this will be waiting for me to say how I never forgave him for his transgression. But that's not the case.

---

[1] Theo Fleury, *Playing with Fire* (HarperCollins Publishers, 2009)

Yes, I was confused and I felt betrayed, hurt and angry. But at the age of 12, I had not yet experienced how other people could support and assist me. At the time, I was terrified to be in the world without my brother and I thought I needed him.

My way of surviving was to keep what had happened a secret. It wasn't that I forgave him; at the time I didn't understand how wrong his behaviour actually was. And I have to remember that he, too, was growing up in the same childhood home as me and I don't think he understood too much about right and wrong, either. Today I forgive the circumstances we were in.

My brother's preoccupation with himself on that day felt similar to what I experienced at the hands of my father. Just as I was afflicted with the same negative characteristics as my mother, including alcoholism, my brother was afflicted with some of the same negative characteristics as my father, including the inability to respect me or my needs. This troubling experience became one of the unwanted memories I stored deep down in the vault of my mind. Before years of therapy helped me bring some resolution to the issue, the memory of it would generate an instant visceral reaction and a psychological shift as soon as it arose. Even today, it is difficult to think about this experience. I feel my mind racing to shift gears to another thought, so I can move away from the emotional pain the memory generates, and this happens so quickly and powerfully I can almost feel my body move physically, as if pulling away. In response to the pain encapsulated within the memory, and to make it through the moment of its existence, I automatically take a deep breath. The memory passes and I carry on.

I wonder how many other women—and men—have secrets like these locked up within their bodies? And what is it going to take to put an end to the abusive behaviour so many thousands of people have experienced silently, somewhere back in their history?

Gratefully, and thanks partly to the writing of this book,

I have finally been able to sit with, and face, many of the challenging memories I had trapped inside me.

I have to admit, when I wrote this chapter I felt concern for what readers might feel towards my brother. What he did was wrong. And he was a young kid trapped in the turbulence created by two parents who were negligent and irresponsible, and who were completely lacking in the ability to provide guidance and correct discipline to their children.

In fact, they were oblivious to what any of us were thinking, doing, or feeling. That doesn't excuse my brother's behaviour. My brother and I shared a secret and I feel compassion for both of our young selves on the day that sorry event took place; my hope is that he will gain relief in its release. The idea that "You're Only as Sick as Your Secrets" is valid and powerful.

Letting it Happen

My second sexual experience occurred at the age of 15 with the first boy who paid me any attention at all.

Up until that point in my life, I had not witnessed, nor had I been taught, what normal, healthy sexual interaction between a boy and a girl looked like. I was confused about it all. Combine that with my low feelings of self-esteem and self-worth, and I see now that I just didn't know any better. So I just let it happen.

There was no romance involved and no real "dating." Nor did The Act even take place in a nice place. In fact, there was nothing remotely comfortable about it. I remember how uncertain and unnerved I felt that day, although this was not an uncommon feeling for me to have. My world had taught me that if I didn't give people what they wanted, or behave as they would have me behave, I would be rejected or abandoned, and I was afraid of that. I did what the boy asked. I took my clothes off, lay down as he requested, and let him have his way with me. That was it. The only feelings or emotions I remember around this experience related to the fact that I was afraid he might not like me if I did not do as he asked. It pains and saddens me greatly to think of how wounded I must have been to accept this as an acceptable sexual experience. In some warped way, I did think that it was okay, and normal. Again, I was unable to say anything … just as I was unable to express aloud to anybody the fact that life around me was scary, confusing, and uncomfortable. Why would I have acted any differently when this situation mirrored the rest of my life? In that moment, all I could do was act like everything was okay. I now know that a lot of young people go through a version of this, and my heart goes out to anyone who has ever felt that they needed to compromise themselves the way I did.

These regrettable, horrible experiences contributed to the shaping of a very damaged young girl. I had very little self-esteem or self-respect, and I felt little self-worth. I have learned to have empathy for the young girl I was, and I have come to know that it is my job on this part of my journey to respect her, and her needs, her wants, her fears, and her perceived inadequacies. Today I am strong enough to look back at myself as a young person with strength, and clarity, and I see my early years through a clear, honest lens. I have been able to access the courage within to see my young self without judgment, and with great compassion. Even though I am so grateful for where I am today, and who I am as a result of all of my experiences, I can't help but wish sometimes that I could just take that young girl in my arms and safely hold her. I want to protect her, respect her and teach her how to value and love herself. Like so many other people, I have been burdened by the secrets of my first sexual experiences—and the shame I felt around them— for most of my life. And relief has come to me through sharing these stories with someone I trusted. If you, too, have some secret stories that are causing you pain, I invite you to reach out to someone experienced in helping people deal with traumatic memories, and put them to rest for once and for all.

Addictive Tendencies

The need to feel different was a strong motivator for me and, from a very young age, I displayed addictive tendencies and behaviours. At around age seven, I found out that I liked the smell and taste of Woodward's Gripe Water. My aunt would give it to my baby cousin to relieve the symptoms of colic, as people often did in those days, and somehow during a visit to my aunt's house, I came to try it. This product was deemed an unapproved drug in the 1990s and banned from import into the USA. It has since been reformulated to contain no alcohol or sugar2 but the original formula that I came to love contained 3.6% alcohol. I remember not only liking the flavour, but also the feeling it gave me. I went back into my niece's room more than once to take a nip, and I drank so much of it, in increments, that my aunt noticed. I remember her saying to my mom that there was quite a bit of it missing— did she think Tina had gotten into it?

Addictive behaviour also showed up when I was 10 years old or so when I went to the Dairy Queen with my brother's baseball team after a game. The parents of one of the boys on the team were treating everyone to banana splits, and I was included in the celebration. I felt lucky that day! I liked the chocolate and strawberry toppings so much that I ate almost all of them right away. I knew before I had finished I wanted more, and I decided it would be a good idea to go back to the counter and say they had not put very much topping on my ice cream and could I please have some more. I remember feeling some shame and embarrassment while standing up there at the ice cream counter asking for more, but it was worth it. Years later I shared this story with my therapist because with its memory I carried shame. Her response was comforting:

"That doesn't surprise me," she said. "Nothing felt good in your world; that did … and you wanted more of it."

---

2 https://en.wikipedia.org/wiki/Gripe_water

That doesn't make the behaviour appropriate, necessarily, but those comments helped me feel less shame and embarrassment whenever that particular memory would arise. Feelings of shame would come up later in life when it came to drinking, particularly around drinking alone, but at the time I would consciously decide it was worth it. My desire to chase the feeling The Drink would give me was greater than my desire to avoid the negative emotion of shame. Today I believe there was not a chance I could have avoided becoming an alcoholic: I witnessed my mother drinking alcoholically for most of my life, and certainly throughout my formative years, and I think there is an element of "monkey see, monkey do" in my behaviour. My mother used alcohol as a coping mechanism, and I did the same. What's more—and this will probably be controversial for some people—I have Native American DNA in my genetic makeup. I am a status Indian by Canadian law and my research, personal experiences, and observations have convinced me alcoholism is common among our country's Indigenous people. Finally, it happened. as I matured, I was so filled with pain and fear from my childhood experiences that all I wanted to do was numb the pain, and shift how I felt; I discovered alcohol was an effective way to do that.

Understanding Alcoholism

With all that as background, I believe no matter how hard I tried, and no matter how much willpower I had, I could not have escaped this disease. I share my experience and the inner workings of my alcoholic brain because I know it is extremely difficult to understand this disease unless you yourself are an alcoholic. Even growing up in an alcoholic home, as so many of us do, was not enough to help me understand alcoholism until I myself succumbed to its clutches. I watched my mother suffer, and I was directly impacted, yet it didn't help me grasp the concept that alcoholism is not at all about choice, and therefore cannot be managed with willpower alone. Throughout my entire childhood, I thought my mother was choosing the bottle over me in the way one would favor one thing over another. I internalized this to mean there was something wrong with me and that my mother didn't love me enough. I have since learned that the disease of alcoholism overrides all power over choice. If you have a loved one who keeps drinking instead of spending time with you, or who fails to follow through on their word, I assure you from experience that it is not because they don't love you. It is because The Drink is making their choices for them. For decades, I saw my mother as being at fault in this, and weak, and I judged her. I really only started to understand when I too became an alcoholic and lived and walked that very same path I had vowed not to follow. I had to feel the impact of the allergy component, go through the cravings, and feel the powerlessness of the Disease myself in order to contradict my own beliefs. Only then did I begin to understand the complete hold alcohol can have on a person. I became the person who reaches shakily over to the bedside table and picks up that early morning drink, knowing full well she won't make it into work again. Only then could I grasp the concept, for some of us at least, drinking alcohol is not a matter of choice. Only when I got sober and could compare my life as an alcoholic with my mother's life as an alcoholic was I able to gain more insight into the Disease and see how malicious the problem of alcohol really is.

I devoted an inordinate amount of time to studying the obsession, compulsion, craving and allergy components of alcoholism, and I combined this knowledge with my experiential understanding of the Disease.

Here is what I've learned:

Nobody chooses to be an alcoholic. When alcohol enters the bloodstream of an alcoholic, something happens that doesn't happen in the average temperate drinker. As the experts at Alcoholics Anonymous say:

"We believe, and so suggested a few years ago, that the

action of alcohol in alcoholics only is a manifestation of an allergy; that the phenomenon of craving is limited to alcoholics as a group and never occurs in the average temperate drinker."[3]

This was written by Dr. William Duncan Silkworth, an American physician who specialized in the treatment of alcoholism. He was the director of the Charles B. Towns Hospital in New York City (NYC) in the 1930s, which is the hospital to which Bill Wilson, Co-founder of AA, was admitted on three occasions. Silkworth was the first to see there was a pathological disease-like basis to alcoholism. He saw it was both an obsession of the mind and an allergy of the body, whereby the obsession compelled people to drink and the allergy condemned the body to go mad or die drinking.[4] There are many who contest the characterization of alcohol as both a disease and an allergy. However, my experience living in the dark tunnel of an alcoholic life has made me feel both of these terms do pretty accurately describe what it's like to be struggling with this cunning, baffling and powerful addiction. One thing all alcoholics have in common an average "problem drinker" does not share is, as stated in the *Big Book of AA*, "They cannot start drinking without developing the phenomenon of craving." The Book further goes on to say,

"This phenomenon as we have suggested may be the manifestation of an allergy, which differentiates these people, sets them apart as a distinct entity. It has never been, by any treatment with which we are familiar, permanently eradicated. The only relief we have is entire abstinence."[5]

Alcoholism as an Allergy

Witnessing my mother's drinking habits while growing up, and knowing my own personal experience of being an alcoholic,

---

[3] Alcoholics Anonymous, "The Doctor's Opinion" in the *Alcoholics Anonymous Big Book* [3] (AABB), 4th Ed (New York, Alcoholics Anonymous World Services, Inc., 2001) p. xxvviii

[4] https://en.wikipedia.org/wiki/Alcoholics_Anonymous

[5] Alcoholics Anonymous, *Alcoholics Anonymous: The Big Book, 4th Edition* P. XXX

I will say that I believe that there is an allergy component with alcoholism. It is a differentiating feature of the Disease and it goes like this: once alcohol enters the bloodstream of an alcoholic, the phenomenon of craving is triggered. Alcoholism is a progressive disease, whereby the intensity of the craving increases over time. In later stages of alcoholism, the craving is so strong words cannot describe it. I know there is literature out there that opposes the idea alcoholism has an allergy component, nor is alcoholism scientifically defined as having one. BUT ...

By definition: An allergy is a chronic condition involving an abnormal reaction to an ordinarily harmless substance called an allergen.[6]

I have lived and experienced alcoholism as being exactly like that definition. The Disease is multi-layered, and complicated, and indeed I believe it includes an allergy component. Think of it this way, if you will: if someone is allergic to peanuts, their body does not typically crave them intensely, nor does their mind claim an obsession and compulsion to eat them. Contrast this with the reaction of a person in later stages of alcoholism, who not only craves the allergen (alcohol), but who also exhibits the mental obsession and compulsion to consume it irrationally. So, imagine being allergic to peanuts, craving them intensely, and also having to battle the obsession and compulsion to eat them, This is alcoholism. Not only do you physically crave something you know is bad for you, but your mind is also obsessed with it and compelled to consume it.

The allergy component over time contributes to the cyclical nature and progression of the Disease, as it fuels the craving. As the allergic reaction increases, so does the craving. So you see, it is not at all a problem of mental control or a perceived

---

[6] Conditions and Treatments of Allergies, America Academy of Allergy, Asthma and Immunology,
https://www.aaaai.org/conditions-and-treatments/conditions-dictionary/allergy.
accessed November 5, 2019

lack of willpower, as many people believe. It is futile to think that high levels of steely-eyed resolve will prevent a person from succumbing to the craving because resolve involves *mental* strength and that is just the point; the craving to pick up drinking again is beyond mental control.

Recently, I was pleasantly surprised by a comment from my optometrist, Dr. Harvey Mayers. He has known me since the very early days of my sobriety and while at my eye examination recently I shared with him the fact that I am an alcoholic who has been eight years sober. He looked at me with curiosity and compassion and he said, "There has to be more to it than just will power." Hallelujah. My response was, "Exactly.

There certainly is and I am hopeful that my book will help create more understanding and awareness around the disease of alcoholism and the world of addictions."

I have never forgotten an AA story I heard once about a businessman who stopped drinking for a few months. He had been working extremely hard on the largest deal of his career and it was due to be secured in just a few days. This man took a drink the day before the deal was to close. Alcohol entered his bloodstream, the phenomenon of craving was triggered and he did not make it the next day to finalize the deal because once he began drinking he didn't stop, and he became a no-show. In a letter to AA in its early days, Dr. Silkworth wrote this: "These men were not drinking to escape; they were drinking to overcome a craving beyond mental control."[7]

I have many personal examples of this mechanism, one of which dates to a time when I had signed up for a yoga teacher training workshop in Hawaii. I had already paid for both my flight and the workshop and I was excited about attending. Yoga training meant a great deal to me and my career, and I was thrilled to be going to Hawaii, a place I had dreamt about

---

[7] Alcoholics Anonymous, *Alcoholics Anonymous: The Big Book,* *4th Edition* P. XXX

visiting for years. I picked up a drink on the Monday before the training. And I didn't stop drinking all week. I had to keep feeding the craving. When it was time to get ready for my flight, I was still intoxicated and too physically ill to change gears and pull myself together. I missed the course and lost the money on my flight. And I kept on drinking.

These examples show a compulsion that is no different than the one at work in a mom who wants and needs to attend her daughter's dance recital. She picks up a drink the night before, sets off the phenomenon of craving, and she doesn't stop drinking. Twenty-two hours after she picks up the first drink she is too drunk to go to the recital. The dance recital mom, the businessman, and me, we all kept drinking to overcome a craving beyond our mental control.

Alcohol Addiction Ruins Lives

While it is tempting to demonize an alcoholic and blame him or her for what might appear to be willfully rotten behaviour, I know of too many intelligent and determined people who have been unable to shake their alcoholism no matter how hard they tried, which supports my contention, and that of many other people—including Dr.Silkworth—that alcoholism is indeed in part an allergy. People of professional standing and good moral character, myself included, have the disease of alcoholism and, as I have suggested, it is the manifestation of an allergy, which triggers the craving and that which differentiates these people. But allergy or not, Alcohol addiction deprives families of the basic necessities of life and it dehumanizes relationships that could otherwise be close, caring and secure. Lives have been ruined, and children have been compromised, and all because we don't understand the choking hold with which this horrible disease of addiction grips those afflicted.

The Question to Ask Yourself:

Do I know enough about alcoholism and addictions to make the judgments I make?

Teen Years. Scenes From a Bad Movie

The vicious hold alcoholism has on its victims casts a long shadow. My parents divorced and I moved in with my mother, who, sadly, was drinking more and more all the time. One day I came home from school and saw through the side door window before I entered the house that a boy who lived in the house across the street was shooting up at our kitchen table. I saw the needle stuck in his arm and the features on his face change as the drugs began to work their way into his system. His brothers were pretty much all drug dealers and he and I had just started to become close. I walked into the house and pretended I hadn't seen anything. I never told anybody what I had seen and I pretended to myself this wasn't one of the most horrifying things I had ever witnessed. It became another secret I locked into the vault of my mind.

You know, some people say everything you go through in life is designed to prepare you for what is coming next. It's a good thing I had already learned some survival skills in my life up until that point, as they were surely needed in helping me deal with what was to come next. As a teenage girl, I had a mother who wasn't the easiest person in the world to live with. As I have now experienced the heartbreak of divorce myself, I can understand the deep pain she must have been going through at the time. Divorce surely is an adversity that gives us either the opportunity to grow or a reason to break. My mother seemed to find in it a reason to break. She was 33 when she and my father split up, and it was the 80s. Sex, Drugs, and Rock'n'Roll pretty much sum up my mother's first year of living as a single woman. The most significant and powerful variable here was, at this point, my mother's alcoholism had progressed to the point where she was drinking daily and although she tried, she was not able to be a mother to me. She experienced a new bottom here as The Drink led her to go into work at the hospital with alcohol in her system and she was fired. This led her deeper into the Disease. Her response to this loss was to drink even more, which made her even less available to me. I was feeling so alone, having been separated from the rest of my family, and although they were a dysfunctional lot, they were all I had. What was worse was the fact that even though I was physically living with my mother, she really wasn't present.

Aspects of this new living arrangement were even more frightening than I'd experienced living in the war zone of my parent's marriage. Throughout the year I lived with my mother after my parents' divorce, I witnessed scenes from what seemed like an ongoing X-rated movie. I felt like I watched this movie alone and there were parts I turned away from and pretended I didn't see.

Every Day Was a Party

I became a little weary and skeptical of the frightening new world into which I had been thrust. I had already been conditioned to live in a scary and uncomfortable home environment, but I was not prepared for the impact that my mother's new level of alcoholic living would have on my life. Every day was a party for my mother now, and drugs and alcohol littered my home while strangers entered and left at all hours. I had no control over my living conditions while, as an adolescent, I was going through many changes, none of which I was prepared for or supported through. I lived through an unimaginable level of daily discomfort and fear during this time. Would there be food in the fridge? Where would I get money? Would strange people party late into the night again tonight? What version of my mother would I meet today? When would I be invited to my dad's house? When would I see my brothers? Will the people in my home when I get there after school make me feel uncomfortable? I never knew what I would come home to or what I would be exposed to when I walked through my own front door. This is a segment of my life that I describe as a bad movie, or something like living in an episode from the television series, *The Twilight Zone*.

A 15-year-old girl should never be in that type of environment, norexposedtoit. Itwasbeyondmycomprehension and I was not equipped mentally or emotionally to handle such difficult circumstances. All I could think of to do was to turn away from it and put on my brave face again. I began to adapt to my surroundings in an almost chameleon-like way. I put on a tough-girl outer shell to help manage the shattered interior that was causing me so much pain. My dress, my speech, my opinions, and my attitudes all took on the abrasiveness of what was going on around me.

I was troubled as I quietly watched my mother have what appeared to be a difficult time getting back on her feet and finding a place in the world as a newly-divorced woman. This is a stressful transition for anybody, but I believe it was even more difficult for her to manage and cope with because of her alcoholism. I do not know if she had any other coping mechanisms to draw on but her choice method seemed to be The Drink. The Drink seemed to have taken my mother from me, and it confused and frustrated me to see her go through this. I was angry at her, and sad for her at the same time. I had zero understanding of the fact that this situation was out of her control. She was fully in the grips of alcoholism, and this is where it got worse.

Stuffing Memories Down

While living with my mother I would almost always come home from school to find her partying. I saw a lot of flirtatious behaviour and illicit drug use, and men who were in my home partying with my mom would look at me in ways that made me feel creepy and awful, different from what I had ever felt before. I had some sense that it was all wrong but I had no clue what to do about it, and nobody to talk to about it. This became all the more confusing for me one day when my mother took me on a double date with her. Her date picked us up and he prepared dinner for us at his home. The disturbing part was that my "date"—this man's younger brother—was still way older than me. This definitely represented questionable behaviour on the part of every adult present. By the grace of God, he was either a decent guy, or I gave off such a strong negative vibe that when my mom disappeared with her date for a while, the brother didn't hit on me. I do remember feeling the need to say out loud to him, "This isn't a date you know." But I couldn't. I said nothing. There was no point complaining to my mother about the situation: I knew she would not remember anything about it anyway, and since she was the one who had set me up in such a fashion I realized that she obviously felt this was all appropriate. My internal compass had an awareness that this scenario was shameful, but my mother didn't show me that she felt that way, too.

But the whole scenario bothered me and I remember feeling angry with my mother for putting me in this situation. Even though this was not my fault, and I hadn't done anything wrong, I felt ashamed in this, as in other situations. All I could do was move away from these powerful emotions, and I learned to stuff them down inside me in order to manage them and attempt to feel better. I have no idea how many others have taken on this unhealthy coping style. I'm sure it is a fairly standard way of dealing with horrible situations.

To this day, I can still see and feel vividly the rooms of the house my mother and I lived in, and I can conjure up countless images of my mother drunk and high as she partied the days away. At this point, not a lot felt good in my world, as it was a scary place that lacked love and affection. I was primed to turn to anyone for affection and whether by default or close proximity I became increasingly close to the 20-year-old drug dealer from across the street; he became my first real boyfriend. I was desperate to be loved and to not feel so alone. This older guy was nice to me and I developed feelings for him; he took care of me at a time when nobody else was making an effort to do so. Nobody once questioned the impropriety of our relationship, and for the most part, I was okay with it, as he did help me at a time when nobody else would. But I knew on some level that there was something wrong with our relationship and this was reinforced each time my boyfriend would drop me off at school. It was right out of a movie where the older bad-boy guy with a car drops the young girl off at high school. It was a movie I desperately wanted to leave.

Eventually, I could no longer handle my mother's noisy and boisterous party house and since I really had nowhere to go, I moved around to the homes of anyone who would allow me to stay with them. First I stayed for a couple of weeks with my closest girlfriend. When I could no longer stay there I called my father to ask if I could come and live with him. To this day, I remember where I was sitting, how I was feeling, and what was said on that phone call. It went something like this:

"Hi Dad, I can't live with mom anymore," I said. "There is too much partying and I have nowhere else to go."

There was a pause and the silence hung in the air.

"You can't come here," he said, along with a couple of other sentences that I no longer remember.

You can't come here.

His refusal to take me in at a time of deep despair generated a huge amount of pain within me that cut deeply and wouldn't leave me. I became even more confused about the world around me and I felt even more insecure about my place within it. The challenge of figuring out how I would find a home was something I was simply not equipped to resolve. But with my father's door closed to me, I called my Aunt Laurie in desperation and I was grateful that she took me in for a time, although it was while living with her that I was to have an encounter that left me even more afraid and confused about my worthiness. As the weeks unfolded, the parents of my aunt's boyfriend showed an interest in taking me in and becoming my guardians. They had the means to do so and they said they were interested in having a foster daughter in their life. I was 16 years old and in Grade 11 by this time.

They invited me to come and spend a weekend with them at their beautiful country home to see how we would get along together, and to determine if we might all feel like it was a good idea for me to live with them on a full-time basis. I arrived on a Friday evening and things started off as a normal series of interactions between an adult couple and a young girl. We sat down to a cheerful dinner before things deteriorated into what would seem to become just like another bad scene in a horrible movie. After dinner, the couple asked me to join them upstairs. The lady proceeded to take me to their bedroom where, unbeknownst to me, her husband was snorting lines of cocaine. I had never tried cocaine before, but I had used other recreational drugs and alcohol. They offered me a line, and I accepted. I think my hope of being welcomed into their family interfered with my ability to wonder why someone would do such a thing. And as a 16-year-old girl, I had been conditioned to accept, if an adult is in charge, what they say goes.

A very large amount of cocaine was put out on the table, and as the evening progressed the man became completely naked and the lady took off her top. Despite feeling unsure and uncomfortable with the situation, I did not leave and proceeded to snort cocaine with them. I remember telling myself that I was okay, that I could handle this, and the troubling part was that despite the numbed-out state I had fallen into, deep down I felt a sad sense of hopelessness that night. In my mind, the intent of the visit had been to see if they liked me and wanted to take responsibility for me. I remember I had been very excited about that weekend, as I thought that this could be my chance to be part of a family. At one point, while the wife left the room to go to the bathroom, the man said words I will never forget, and which still scare me today.

"I will put another pile of cocaine out if you take your top off."

Tapping into a Protective Spirit

I haven't said much about my spiritual beliefs to this point but like many people who have had to deal with the unthinkable in their lives, I have become a deeply spiritual person. I believe I have been guided and protected and there were many times when a simple change of one detail in a specific scenario—such as the one I've just described—could have resulted in a far worse outcome, or even death. What happened that night with the people who had pretended to want to take care of me is what I believe is an example of the spiritual energy that surrounded me at times like a protective barrier; for some reason, I didn't take my top off. I said "no," and shortly after that I went to bed alone feeling ashamed, disappointed, and defeated. And on some level, I also felt violated.

What hurt the most about this evening was that my hopes of feeling wanted and finding a home had been demolished. I had thought I might have found a family. What I found instead were two predatory adults with no boundaries and no sense of integrity. I am so grateful the situation didn't deteriorate. There was a fallout, however, as I struggled with the memories of that evening. I carried a lot of shame and the whole series of events around this couple became another secret that I tucked away deep inside the vault of my mind.

After a few months of living with my aunt, I decided to move in with my boyfriend the drug dealer. He lived with his father and three brothers, who were also drug dealers. This new living arrangement was grossly wrong on so many levels, but for me, at the time, it was just another decision that I had to make. I didn't see that I had much choice, and I knew it was inappropriate, but I was only trying to survive and I was out of options. Thinking back to this time in my life I so wish that I had parents who were well enough to step in and protect me. I wish that I had not been placed in such a scenario where accepting this living arrangement was my best option. I believe this was the most difficult and painful period of my life. I felt abandoned and neglected by the people who were supposed to love me and take care of me. I believe that some kind of energy protected and cared for me, preventing an even worse outcome. Grace was with me.

One Foot in Front of the Other

I now had a permanent address, and the stress of wondering where I would put my head at night—and the weight of not really feeling at home—was lifted to some degree. But other struggles remained. It seemed like everyone around me was having a hard time making ends meet. My mother had lost her job, and I couldn't count on my father for support as he failed to follow through on his obligation to pay the court-ordered $20 a week he was supposed to be giving me. I never pursued my parents or held them accountable for their actions, but instead, I took on a part-time job working 24 hours a week after school and on weekends to provide for myself and help my boyfriend's family with the cost of food and shelter. I worked as a telephone solicitor and it was a pretty good job that served me well, as it paid more than McDonald's did. But I did resent it. I envied most of the other kids engaging in after school activities while I went off to work. I wasn't buying the latest pair of sneakers with my hard-earned cash. My work life was about survival. Everyone has their own journey, and this was mine. Ultimately, it would all benefit me in life, but it sure didn't seem like it at the time.

Despite my tumultuous and precarious living conditions, I continued to go to high school and ultimately managed to graduate. I felt a huge disconnect in living with a drug dealer in a five-man home while trying to be a Grade 11 student at high school and hold down a part-time job. I would go to school and while there I would feel the sense of being young and, for brief flashes of time, I felt almost carefree as I felt the goodness and the accomplishment of learning. I loved learning, and I still do. It injects me with purpose and worth and I love that feeling. After school, I would go to work and feel good about myself while I was there, too. But as soon as I went home to where I lived, I didn't feel good at all. Actually, it was kind of disgusting. And I don't even know how to describe how I felt being such a young girl and having to exist amongst so many older men. A few days a week I would pick up groceries and cook dinner for my boyfriend, his father and myself. It was my way of earning my keep and it felt good to do so.

When the weather would allow it, we would put our milk and the odd groceries on the window sill, because if we put them in the fridge, they would be gone when we went back to get them.

I am embarrassed to share the details of how I had to live during this time, just as I was a little afraid at the time that somebody would find out. There was a dirty feel to who I had to be in order to fit into this home and there was literally a dirty feel to the house itself because it was rarely cleaned. There was no shower in this home, and I would have to wash the bathtub before I bathed because it was so grimy. And even after I bathed there was still a sense of dirtiness in my world and in me.

But, honestly, through it all, the thing is, I was good with this, this was my lot and I knew I had to figure things out. There were moments of light in my life that seemed holier and cleaner than the world around me and sometimes it would shine through me. And then I would have odd moments of self-care and a recognition of boundaries. I hadn't really experienced or internalized what it was like to have a caring parent, so I didn't have a lot of wisdom around what self-care was. The fact that no serious harm came to me during this time is proof to me again that God's Grace had placed its protective force around me.

I lived in the drug dealers' house for about a year and during that time I grew up a lot. By the time of my 17th birthday, I was certainly mature and worldly beyond my years. Survival had become my watchword. I had witnessed how people lived when they were involved primarily in drugging, drinking, and drug dealing, and I think this experience and awareness of the world helped me to learn that I wanted something different, something more for myself, because I didn't like what I saw.

Up until this point I had dabbled in and experimented with drugs and alcohol more than most young people my age, which was not surprising, given how readily available it all was, how uncomfortable my world was, and the addictive tendencies I was already displaying.

But eventually, while living with my boyfriend and his family, I developed an aversion to drugs and alcohol, and simply stopped using them. I am not sure exactly what led me to this point, but I believe it may have been partly because I was disgusted with what was going on around me. More than that, I am inclined to believe that the grace of God was once again acting as my protective barrier against all things unsavory and dangerous, protecting me and guiding me through this traumatic passage of my life.

During the months that lived with my boyfriend's family, I continued to attend school, work part-time, and read a lot of books. I did my best to improve the circumstances of my life and the situation I was in.

I am sure I enjoyed reading for the escape it provided. It allowed me to get out of my own life, and out of my own head. I spent five years with this boyfriend altogether, during the last four of which we had our own apartment.

I finished high school and, eventually, I grew strong enough to break up with him and start living on my own. It was scary, but I think that looking ahead at the life I was likely to have with my boyfriend was an even scarier prospect.

Living on My Own

My life on my own involved more school. Even though admission requirements were tough, I applied for and was accepted into the three-year Medical Laboratory Technology Program at Mohawk College. I worked and studied hard during my early twenties and had limited finances and very little free time; it meant I rarely drank at all. I was starting to feel better about myself as I moved ahead in acquiring an education, and for the first time in my life, I had a little bit of hope for my future. A sense of excitement was brewing inside me that signaled that maybe life could be all right. At the same time, deep down in the fibre of my being, I was always worried and concerned about my drinking. The fear of becoming an alcoholic like my mother plagued me. The first time I had ever drunk alcohol I drank too much and it worried me. As I grew older and drank on the odd occasion, I would always drink just a little too much and my memory would be fuzzy; this, too, would worry me but I kept it a secret. Even then, I knew there was something different about how I drank. I told no one.

At college, I worked hard. My life was shaping up nicely and I started telling myself that maybe I wasn't an alcoholic after all. Maybe I could still turn this around. On the verge of graduation I could see that I was about to become a professional and I would be earning a decent living; how could I be an alcoholic, I reasoned? Yet deep down inside, I lived with the secret burning knowledge that I was one. Everything came to a head upon my graduation when the excitement of that wonderful day was spoiled for me forever by my alcoholism. I had been working at a bar while going to school and I could not get the Saturday night off on the day of my graduation. It wasn't really that big of a deal, as it was an afternoon convocation and I needed the money. So my plan was to attend the graduation ceremony, have an early celebratory dinner, and then head into the club afterward and do my shift. I will never forget how proud I felt standing there listening to the applause directed at my graduation class.

The program was very difficult and the auditorium erupted in recognition of the stamina and determination of those who had made it through. It was so special. My mother and brother were also in attendance for this hard-won milestone in my life. After a celebratory dinner, which of course included a couple of glasses of wine, I happily went into work.

High on the wine, I had consumed, and on the excitement of my graduation, I then proceeded to have one too many celebratory shots of Grand Marnier with some of the customers who were sitting at the bar that night. By the end of my bar shift, I drank myself into a blackout and lived for the first time with the fear, guilt, and remorse of what I had done. I had no idea how bad my behaviour had been or if I was going to be fired.

This would mark the beginning of countless lapses of memory and the misery that ensued in the wake of an alcoholic blackout. Luckily for me, Francine, the lady I had been working with that evening, covered for me by not making a big deal of it and because I was such a good employee—always on time and good at sales—the incident flew under the radar.

Thank God and thank Francine. I needed that job, as it wasn't just a bar job, it was by far the highest-paying bar job in the city. Despite this troubling incident, I still hung on to the hope that I wasn't a "real alcoholic," that I was not like my mother, and that I could beat it. I clung to the idea that I was different, smarter, and better ... which, of course, I was not.

If Only I Felt Less Pain

I also held to the delusional hope that if only I felt less pain inside then maybe I could drink like a normal person. But, there was no running away from the truth. Each time I drank I noticed a subtle feeling that something just wasn't right. Maybe it was in the way I was obsessed with always—and I mean always—making sure I did not miss last call, making sure I *always* got that last drink … or two.

After I graduated from the Medical Laboratory Technology program, the government at the time instituted some health care cutbacks, which meant there were no jobs available for new graduates. Even though I was a student lab technologist at a clinical hospital, and next in line to be hired, I didn't get a job in my chosen field. I called it a "tough life hit," as I really could have used that job and the pay that came along with it. I felt I had earned it, after all. I felt defeated for a while, but my Inner Spirit Drive propelled me forward and I am grateful today that this experience did not stop me from doing the next right thing, which was to go back to school to train as a nurse. But alcoholism is a progressive disease and a few years had gone by, during which time my Disease, unbeknownst to me, had worsened. Well into the nursing program I was regularly drinking heavily on the two or three days a week that I had off. Drinking was still a lot of fun at this time and it was well worth accepting the minor blips, transgressions, or short term memory losses that were happening, or so I told myself. But, honestly, it wasn't all bad. In my spare time, I would push my fears of being an alcoholic aside and I would just enjoy life. I spent a lot of time with my younger brother, Paul, and his buddy, Brent. Although drinking was part of everything we did, these were two of the happiest years of my life. Paul and Brent were the most fun-loving, charismatic guys you would ever meet. And, oh my God, funny—we laughed so much! I cared deeply for them both and there was a lot of love between us. I will always cherish my time spent with the two of them. My heart warms when I think of those days, and I am grateful for them.

The problem still remained that my drinking was becoming more and more of a problem. The scales weighing the good against the bad were tilting further. And they weren't in my favor.

The intelligent part of the Disease, the part that is an evil demon—the part that is the reason why the Big Book calls this disease "cunning"—was telling me it was no big deal, and that the benefits outweighed the risks. But the adverse effects alcohol was having on my mental and physical body were increasing incrementally over time. The hangovers, which are really mild states of alcohol withdrawal—showed up as dehydration, headaches, and nausea. I started struggling with performance anxiety that manifested as shakes and tremors during my clinical days at the hospital, as well. I was having trouble charting legibly and I was constantly worried that I would have to draw a medication up out of a bottle with a syringe in front of somebody and that they would see my hands shake.

As a rule, I would not go out drinking on clinical nights, because I was afraid of how shaky I might be when I woke up. Despite my efforts to control my drinking I was beginning to drink more often, and consuming more each time, and this is the point where I think my allergy to alcohol was beginning to develop. I had begun to feel, physically, the effects of a night of drinking. When I woke up in the morning I began noticing that in addition to the hangover, my nervous system felt frenzied, as if it were in a constant state of anxiety.

What should have been such an exciting phase of my life was instead a time of great turmoil. I was close to graduating from nursing school and I was ready to start the next chapter of my life, but I was consumed with keeping a lid on my alcoholism. I desperately wanted my story to be different from my mother's, so much so that I willed the tremors to be a result of anxiety, not alcohol withdrawal. My efforts to prove that I had anxiety, and was not an alcoholic, led me to the Anxiety Disorder Clinic at McMaster University.

My hope was that the clinic would give me some magical method to stop the minor tremors and shakes I was experiencing.

But, of course, it was no use, and I can see in hindsight that if I had been truthful and looked at my pattern of drinking, and the anxiety/shakes I was experiencing, it would have been blatantly obvious that my drinking was causing my problems.

The one and only thing that would have helped me with my anxiety disorder at that time would have been to stop drinking. It was The Drink that was causing the anxiety. One hundred percent.

This could have been a moment of truth for me. Like my mother and many others like us, I was no match for the disease of alcoholism. Actually, nobody is. Everything I had fought so hard to overcome, accomplish and become was now about to be torn down and lost at the hands of alcoholism as the Disease progressed within me. The Disease had found me.

The Question to Ask Yourself:
Did I avoid taking responsibility for any addictions I may have had by choosing instead to believe it was anxiety, depression, or a coping mechanism?

5

The Pretend Years. "No, I'm Not an Alcoholic!"

From a young age, I'd vowed I'd never be like my mother. Up until my late twenties I really did believe that if I didn't want to be like her, I could simply choose a different path. The problem, as it turned out, was that I had no choice. The sad truth is that as I grew older, my body's physical and mental response to alcohol changed continually. By the time I was 35, I began to notice that each time alcohol entered my bloodstream, the self-control I did have over my thoughts and behaviours while drinking was unceasingly slipping away from me, one little degree at a time.

The really scary part was that I knew this was happening. And I was powerless to prevent it. I felt like I was living out some kind of sentence of doom, and I was also beginning to process that things were only going to get worse. I felt the fear of this stark reality, and yet I just turned away and carried on. Some people may feel that this was a point at which I could have turned things around or stopped the progression of the Disease, and, yes, I agree—it was. The problem was that I knew nothing about this disease except what I had gleaned from experience. I felt all this, and on some level, I knew this, but a part of me was utterly confused by it all, as I had never talked with another alcoholic or heard one share anything similar; hence I easily slipped into delusion.

And so the Disease continued to progress in me.

It was at about this stage of becoming an alcoholic myself that I began to understand why my mother drank instead of showing up for me throughout my childhood years. In fact, she hadn't chosen at all. It was the alcoholic part of my mother who chose alcohol over me. My mother had been powerless. I was now starting to experience the same powerlessness. Despite strength of my desire to *not* be like my mother, the Disease had progressed in me to a point where it was obvious that I was indeed just like her. For the next decade or so, I secretly drank alcoholically while pretending to the world that I was okay. It was not unlike I had been as a child when I pretended to be fine while my world crashed and burned around me. The stakes were much higher now. My very life was at stake.

Damaged and Delusional

One serious — though somewhat dysfunctional — relationship I had in my early thirties ended somewhat amicably, although I was struck by the last thing that my partner said to me as I walked out the door.

"You won't find anyone else to love you, the way you drink," he said.

His words hung heavily in the air, because they were true, and they left a lasting impression. They were the very first acknowledgment out loud, the first verbal outing, of the fact of my drinking problem. The statement both hurt and scared me very much and in some way it may have been the first time I really and truly felt like an alcoholic. I was desperate to keep that information quiet. So I did all I could do at the time and that was to not address it at all and so I became an alcoholic-in-hiding.

I went back to living in the delusion that I could beat this disease and someday drink like a normal person. I went back to holding onto the hope that someday I would not hurt so much from the pain of my childhood, that I could escape this disease of alcoholism and one day drink with impunity. Had a Genie popped out of a bottle and offered me three wishes I would have only needed two: one would be to free me of the emotional pain I felt and the second would be to allow me to drink. I know it seems ludicrous to think, if a person were granted Genie wishes, they would use one to be able to drink. I know it may be hard for non-alcoholics to understand how important The Drink is to those who have the allergy and craving. But I can't explain it; sometimes it is all that matters. By now I had started to live in the fear that I might not be able to beat this. I was now starting to feel the powerlessness I had seen my mother live out in her own life. All the years I had spent telling my mother to just stop drinking played repeatedly in my mind. I felt like, and lived, as though alcohol were the only way for me to cope with what I was feeling. At this point, I thought that I would either find a way to manage, or I would die trying. There was no third option labelled "give it up." Because the problem with giving it up meant I had to start feeling and stop avoiding the pain. I had to begin to sit and be with the pain. I had to not numb myself with alcohol. Numbing myself with alcohol meant I wasn't able to work through anything. All The Drink did was postpone the process. I had to face my demon of alcoholism head-on and feel the pain that was inside me. I had to stop drinking my pain away. To do this I would have to learn new coping mechanisms and even before that, I had to face the truth that I was an alcoholic. That was the first step. Like many others who have been in my shoes, this is a tall order, and one that I was not yet ready to do. Despite the pain and all of the struggles that had now become part and parcel of my drinking, I was not ready to quit. All I was ready for was to continue trying to keep drinking. I was just not ready to face the aching pain inside of me that I was desperately trying to move away from—the pain that I still desperately hoped would magically dissipate if I could only find love. The love of a good partner would surely fix me, or so I thought. It seems like a preposterous idea now that I look back knowing what I know.

I have since come to learn that nothing external and nobody other than me could have mended or healed what was broken inside of me. All the fixing had to be done by me. The Disease of alcoholism had derailed my thinking in so many ways. I was delusional to think that I could ignore my alcoholism and that my life would still turn out as I had planned. I was delusional to think that I was different or smarter than my mother had been and that I would be able to beat this disease. I thought the rules of this life didn't apply to me, which turned out to be an idea stemming from my weaker self's decision to listen to my ego. More delusion. I mean, many of us at one time or another have been in a situation in life where we thought or hoped the rules didn't apply to us. I learned they do! Nobody is exempt. Eventually, absolutely everything catches up. I honestly wanted to believe that somehow, someway my demon of alcoholism could be — Poof! — Gone!

NOT.

How many times have we seen people who have every aspect of their lives in order, except for one area of neglect? Let's take a successful 60-year-old businessman. He has a great marriage and kids, brilliant career, many friends, and enough financial wealth to be able to afford a life of luxury and privilege. The piece that he has not taken care of is his health. Despite warnings and a family history of cardiac disease, he thinks he is exempt from danger. But the runway runs out for him and he drops dead of a heart attack. The lesson for all of us is that all areas of our lives must be in order. I was guilty of thinking I, too, was exempt. I thought keeping all the other aspects of my life in order would cover the slack for the area that was not: my alcoholism. Other people have different areas of neglect, like uncontrolled diabetes, high cholesterol, overspending, weight problems, overwork. Or maybe the area of neglect is time spent … maybe away from work, maybe with your children. We all have an area that has room for growth.

Dressing up and Hiding

I deluded myself into thinking that I could dress myself up and hide, or ignore my alcoholism and think I could get away with it. I mean, after all, I had worked hard to build myself a life and I had a lot to offer; I should be able to match up with a good partner and get on with the rest of my life. I was so sorely mistaken. Here was another myth of youth and ignorance. The area that is not in order in an individual's life will eventually either come back to haunt you or come back to bite you in the ass. I did not want to believe this, but it's true. I thought I could escape the truth about my alcoholism and its ramifications, but I could not, it just doesn't work that way. The problem: I wasn't ready to face the truth. I think this was mostly because I was not ready to give up the drinking. I knew that once I admitted I was an alcoholic and tried to stop drinking, the game would be over. No longer would I be able to hang with my buddy The Drink. So I carried on, hiding how much I really drank from everyone who knew me.

The people I drank with almost never knew how many drinks I had before I even started to drink with them. I would drink before I met up with people, I would drink while I was out with them and I would always drink more when I got home. I was always working to get myself to the point where I couldn't feel anything and I would drink away what I was feeling and chase the numb state. In my final years of heavy drinking, it became an all-consuming goal to make sure I always had enough to consume, no matter what I was doing, so that I'd be able to drink like I wanted to. Sometimes it seemed like it was all I thought about. For example, while out on a date at a nice restaurant for Sunday Brunch one day I excused myself to visit the bathroom and on the way back to my table I stopped and quickly grabbed a shot of Grand Marnier at the bar. I hated how this made me feel, but I couldn't stop myself.

Sometimes I'd start off an evening drinking with my sophisticated professional friends, only to engage in part two of the evening with people who drank as I did. Or, as was the case more often, in the end, I'd mostly drink at home in isolation. I felt a lot of shame and self-loathing around the secret way in which I was drinking and it was tearing me up inside. I felt like I was leading a double life, one as an ICU nurse, and the other as an alcoholic. The person I was while I was drinking alcoholically was almost unrecognizable to the person I was when I was abstaining and working as a nurse. The sicker my alcoholism made me, the more secrets I had to keep.

Finding Partners in Life

When it comes to finding partners in life, you certainly are drawn to people with an equal number of issues, or roughly the same number of "Samsonite bags" as you have, but they are not necessarily in the same category as the ones you are dragging around with you. Energetically, I have come to see that we tend to attract a person who is equally messed up, and that's what I did. I was so wrong to think my demons wouldn't affect who I would choose to partner up with. I thought I could wrap myself up in nice clothes like a bow and present myself to the world while hiding my demons and character defects. As much as I tried, I certainly learned that really, truly, there is no getting away from what is below the surface and on the inside. What I portrayed myself to be on the outside was barely even a skin-deep reflection of who I truly was. Once alcohol was added to the matrix, I became a different person, the Alcoholic Tina, whose demons and defects were part and parcel of who she truly was. The last serious relationship I had before crashing was with a man I met while traveling in Las Vegas. I ended up marrying him. What started off as a strong connection with just the touch of a hand and one look from his piercing sea-blue eyes on my last night in Vegas turned into a bad Danielle Steele novel.

We both entered our marriage in hopes of being exempt from our demons and neither of us was forthcoming about them at the outset. I moved from Toronto to St. Louis to be with this man. I knew only him when I moved there in hopes of starting a new life. I easily found a job working as a nurse, as I already held all the required paperwork needed for a Canadian nurse to cross the border and work in the United States. I was lucky! Well, actually, not so lucky, as these turned out to be the loneliest and darkest times I had ever known. I felt the same longing for affection and love I had felt as a child but it was magnified by feelings of desperation and disappointment that stemmed directly from my ill-advised marriage.

I was so wrong to think a geographical change and this relationship would fix all my problems and take away my pain. It actually did the opposite. I don't want to lay any more fault with him than I deserve myself, but I believe my husband struggled with his own inner conflict, as he was not sure of his identity, or who he really wanted to be. Because of this, he was not able to be there for me physically, mentally or emotionally, which left me painfully lonely and isolated, almost entirely alone with my own inner conflict, The Drink. I have to share this. When I hear of people who cancel or back out of upcoming nuptials, I envy their courage. I knew going into this marriage that it was wrong and that it would not work. My instincts were screaming at me to not go through with it and there were blatant warning signs that all would not be well. But I did not listen and went ahead on the strength of the delusion that it *might* work. I mean, the invitations had been sent out. How I wish I had had the courage to be truthful and make the tough decision that was best for both of us in the long term.

The marriage ended abruptly and to this day, I feel sadness for the pain we caused each other. He was a special man. When thoughts of him enter my mind, I hope that he did indeed find his true self. The impact of the breakup catapulted me into a sea of pain, deeper than the ocean of his eyes, and I escalated my drinking in my efforts to cope. Drinking remained the only way I knew how to deal with pain.

The pain and heartbreak of yet another failure and the fact that alcoholism is a progressive disease pushed me deeper into its depths and things got much worse. The six years following the breakup with my husband were ruled by the Drink. I began to spiral out of control. During this time I think the Disease in me was progressing rapidly. The part of me that sensed what was happening also felt the terror of my situation. It was kind of like the pace of my descent into annihilation had changed; I felt as if I were trying to walk through quicksand. I have heard people share that going through a painful or traumatizing experience can rapidly intensify the pace of the Disease's progression, particularly in women. I think that was the case with me. Even though I knew I was free-falling, I still could not see or fathom a life without the relief of The Drink. It is hard to explain to a normal drinker how an alcoholic cannot envision a life without sitting on patios, sipping cocktails, hearing the clink of the glass ... and the "glorious" lifestyle that goes along with it all. When you are in the grips of this disease, you cannot see a life without it. It is an absurd and mind-warping obsession. For an alcoholic, alcohol literally becomes your best friend. To imagine this friend forever removed from your life just does not compute. It is unfathomable. We do not want to experience life without it.

This helps explain why giving up one's addictive substance is so very difficult, especially in the beginning; it involves a painful grieving process. Drinking had become my everything; my whole world revolved around it, and The Drink had become my best friend, my relief, my way to cope. In the end, it became my way to live.

The Abnormal Became My Normal

Normal drinkers can use The Drink to cope, enhance social engagements, and get relief. In the end—for me at any rate—grabbing a drink on the way home from work or while at a bar didn't mean anything social, in fact, it was a risky business. What I was risking by picking up that first drink was my job, my relationships, my reputation, my health, pieces of my soul, and potentially my life. At this stage of the progression of my Disease, each time I drank, would lead to another series of binge drunks ahead that would include drinking myself into oblivion, and yet another string of blackouts. After each blackout, I would awaken to the sinking, dreadful feeling deep in my soul that I'd lost another piece of myself. In AA we are reminded that when we're tempted to pick up a drink we should "follow the train wreck" that will happen as a result all the way to the last station. This is what AA calls a "Remember When" moment. It prompts us to vigilantly and continuously keep in mind the truth of how bad our drinking really is. The human mind will always need reminders.

This is similar to when a girl breaks up with her boyfriend because he is physically and emotionally beating her. After a couple of days, the young girl starts missing the sweet things about him and starts to forget how hard he had been hitting her. Then, after a few more days or weeks, the young girl starts pining for him, and she starts missing the gifts he gave her and the dinners he treated her to that made her feel special ... but she forgets that he always told her she was no good. She forgets the slaps, the punches, the insults, the complaints.

It's so easy as humans for our minds to fall prey to the delusional thought it will be different this time, or even romanticize it will be better.

As described in The Big Book:

"The idea that somehow, someday he will control and enjoy his drinking is the great obsession of every abnormal drinker. Many pursue it to the gates of insanity or death." [8]

What is an Alcoholic Blackout?

By this point, I was experiencing an alcoholic blackout almost every time I drank and I have some strong and disturbing memories of observing my mother in what I believe to be blackouts as well. They are part of the evolution and progression of the Disease. According to the National Institute on Alcohol Abuse and Alcoholism, a blackout is a state where

---

[8] Alcoholics Anonymous, *Alcoholics Anonymous: The Big Book,* *4th Edition,* p.30

a person is not in control of their thoughts or actions and has little control over their emotions and impulses.[9] Blackouts are not at all like passing out. If you are passed out, you are in a deep sleep state. If you are in a blackout, you're walking and talking.

While in an alcoholic blackout, a person will have no recollection at all of the events that occurred over a period of time, ranging from several minutes to several hours. They don't remember what happened to them, or what they have done. While in a blackout, the person is drunk and walking and talking but the alcohol in their system has turned off the recording part of their brain. Blackouts are not limited to alcoholics, as they may happen for a shorter time frame in someone who may have consumed alcohol too quickly on an empty stomach, as often happens to teenagers experimenting with alcohol. An alcoholic in a blackout state is capable of unimaginable behaviour that is far from their norm.

Shocking though it may seem, I personally have experienced—and survived—hundreds of blackouts of varying degrees of severity over the course of my 25 years of drinking. This is deeply disturbing to me. On one occasion I went out drinking with a friend and responsibly took a taxi both to and from the downtown bar where we met. I remember the taxi ride home and the one last glass of wine I sat down with when I got in. I thought this would be a safe and responsible way to drink, at home and behind closed doors. Did I ever think wrong? Despite how responsibly I felt I had been drinking, I slipped into another blackout. The sad and disturbing truth is that, while in this blackout, I proceeded to get into my car in an extremely intoxicated blackout state and drive two blocks up the street to the gas station. I filled my car with gas and drove away without paying. Why I chose to do this is a mystery, as

---

[9] Aron M. White, "What Happened? Alcohol, Memory Blackouts, and the Brain," National Institutes on Alcohol Abuse and Alcoholism, 2003 https://pubs.niaaa.nih.gov/publications/arh27-2/186-196.htm Accessed November 4, 2019

I did not actually need any gas at the time. The only reason I know I did this was because I got a call from a police officer working in the division where I lived the next day. I did not answer his call, but he left me a message telling me the gas station attendant had captured my license plate number and that I had driven away without paying for my gas. I went in the next day and paid the amount owed, pretending it had been an oversight. It was a humiliating and shameful experience. But this seems like a small price to pay for my actions when compared with how things would have rolled out if I had killed others or myself.

It is horrifying to consider how much time I must have spent in blackouts with no memory of what I did or said. These memories affect me to this day and I feel a huge amount of pain, anxiety, and remorse over my behaviour. Sometimes I feel guilty that worse things didn't happen to me, as I know countless others were not so lucky and were not spared. Once again, I feel that my protective barrier was at work on my behalf, taking care of me.

Things could have been very different for me. My hope is that by sharing this information readers may be more informed about how an alcoholic blackout can have detrimental and everlasting effects that can change people's lives forever.

The Question to Ask Yourself:
Are self-pity, denial, self-doubt, fear, addiction, overeating, overspending or any other unhealthy behaviours holding me back or limiting me from reaching my potential.

6

My Final Drinking Years.
A Game of Russian Roulette

I named my final few years of drinking the Russian Roulette Years because drinking had become a high-risk activity. Every time I drank I might lose anything from some of my belongings and my integrity, to my life itself. My drinking had progressed to the end stages of alcoholism; it had become potentially very dangerous. If I woke up from a night of drinking and I was home alone and uninjured in my bed, with my cell phone, purse, and jacket all with me, I considered it to have been a good night of drinking. I am not saying that this was good behaviour, nor am I condoning it. But in order to drink, I had to accept the risks involved. I had to accept new lows and new bottoms while turning a blind eye to my behaviour because I felt so degraded. Each time I awoke after a night of drinking I would mentally and physically cringe, swallow hard at my reality and push the thoughts of who I was becoming or what I was doing to myself away. I hated myself for accepting this way of life, but I didn't see any way out, because I could not fathom giving up The Drink. I needed it! Or so it felt.

As time went on, I began to accept more and more highly abnormal and detrimental behaviours to accommodate my alcoholic drinking. I know they may seem pathetic or even outrageous, but they demonstrate how we alcoholics are driven to insanity to keep drinking. And that is the exact point; we will do anything to drink. I think most of us who are alcoholic slowly and incrementally, over time, degree by degree, lower the standard of what we accept of ourselves, of those around us and of our lives in general. People from all walks of life come to their version of a bottom and for most people that revolves around whatever standard will allow them to continue to drink. Why would I ever accept not knowing where I was when

I would wake up? The reason: because I had no choice but to accept this. Because what I couldn't do was give up drinking.

For example, I started leaving my condo door unlocked if I went out drinking because nine times out of ten I would return in a blackout, and I would be unsure of my surroundings. I'd cause a ruckus and disturb my neighbours. One evening I became so disruptive that I received a letter from the board of my condominium's management company warning me to conduct myself appropriately in the building's public areas while intoxicated. It stated that if I weren't able to do so, the police would be called. Apparently, while I had been in an alcoholic blackout a few nights earlier, my neighbours had called security after I tried to gain entry into another unit in the building I had thought was my own. I had banged on more than one door that night, one of which was not even on the same floor as my unit. I have no recollection of this at all and I was aghast when I read this letter. I was filled with shame and all I wanted to do was crawl into a hole and die. The humiliation and embarrassment that I felt were horrible and it lingered. I was left forever wondering who may have seen me, what was being said about me, and what people thought about me. This kind of incident is an example of how we alcoholics can get to a point where we feel we have to drink to deal with the shame, guilt, and remorse that has cropped up in the wake of our most recent bout of drinking. At times I would see that the only way out of the dark place I had drunk myself into was to numb myself into oblivion again. Over and over again, I would awaken in the morning with the same mixture of emotions eating away at me and weighing me down. I would allow consciousness to surface enough for me to feel the torment of these emotions, and they were just as heavy in my mind as they were in my heart. I felt cornered and weighted down, smothered by the pressure of the thoughts that burdened me. It is really difficult to think back to those times and see how I put myself in harm's way to the point my intoxication rendered me capable of waking up in bed with a stranger. I own it, I brought it on myself. I am not saying there is anything wrong with consensual sex, but I know there were times when I wished there would have been someone there to help me. The truth is what would have helped me most was to not have been drunk enough to blackout in the first place. I was far away from my true essence at this point, completely disconnected from my spirit, and floundering amidst the pain and chaos I called life. Some of these experiences still haunt me today.

Progressive Disease: Day Drinking

In the very first moment of consciousness every morning, I would do a tally of possible damages that I had done while drinking the night before. I wanted badly to stuff my thoughts down and away because coming out of a drunken haze was always a slow and scary process. I would hold my breath while I assessed the possible ramifications of my behaviour. First, I would check where I was, if I were alone, and whether I was hurt. Next, I would try to think about what day it was. Had I missed work? What responsibility was I shirking? Jagged and deep breaths would be required to make it through this initial fact-checking process. It was at this phase of my alcoholism the insatiable need to feed the craving to drink inside of me became so strong that I crossed another line. The crossing of this new line would bring me to a new level of drinking that included drinking in the morning or what some would call day drinking.

At At this phase of my drinking, if I woke up and there was alcohol in the condo (or wherever I was when I woke up), I would drink. If there happened to be wine left in the glass on the bedside table, I would be compelled to reach over and pick it up. Sometimes I would reach for it and down it quickly just so I would ward off any feeling at all, so I could maintain the numbness my mind and body so desperately needed and wanted. I wanted to quell my mind, and I needed to pacify the craving of my addiction. The relief I felt around the thought of The Drink, the taste of The Drink and the feeling of alcohol again entering my system was powerful and I became to need it more and more. No words can describe what I was now going through except despair. It was physical and mental misery. If I woke up and there was nothing to drink in my condo, I would often call a bottle service for a delivery because they were open 24 hours a day. The reason dial-a-bottle services are open 24 hours a day is to meet the needs of people—primarily alcoholics—who run out of booze when the liquor store is closed. If I were sober enough I would drive to the nearest liquor store, because that was the quickest way to get my hands on a bottle of alcohol. When I say the quickest way, I am trying to share and explain that while the Disease progresses, drinking becomes much more than relief, it becomes a need. Which touches on another point a lot of people don't realize is that alcoholism is a progressive disease. What this typically means is that over time, the hold or the grip the disease has on each alcoholic becomes worse. For me, this meant that I was drinking larger quantities and I was drinking more often. The craving increased and my control over it decreased. The progression I speak of is invisible and unstoppable. You might wish that if you stopped drinking for a month or a year, you could resume drinking as if time away from The Drink rendered you less of an alcoholic. Maybe you could reverse the progression, reverse the stages of the Disease, or maybe you could magically bring yourself to a place where you could at least have a couple of drinks now and again. But it doesn't work that way. It is the exact opposite. I will never forget the chilling statement someone shared with the group while I was in treatment.

"While you are in here abstaining from The Drink, your Disease is in the parking lot doing pushups."

Sadly, I can attest this statement is 100 % accurate.

Keeping The Disease At Bay

Often I would wake up with nothing in the house to drink

because, during the last year or two of this madness, I would purposefully only pick up enough for a daily drunk, in hopes that I wouldn't drink the following day. When I say, "in hopes," I am trying to say I made desperate attempts to save myself. In fact, for years, I fought for my life. Unbeknownst to anybody who knew me, I tried everything to control my drinking, limit my drinking or stop my drinking. Yet no matter how hard I tried or how I thought I might outsmart it, it had me beat. I put forth painstaking efforts to not go down the alcoholic path that glared ahead of me.

In my early thirties, one of my valiant attempts to control my drinking led me to take Antabuse. Antabuse, also called Disulfiram, is a prescription medication that has always been controversial because it is essentially a poison and if taken with alcohol it makes you violently ill. It can even lead to death. When I was a child my uncle had taken Antabuse and he was able to get sober for a little while with its help. I also remember my mother being on it as well. One day she was drunk and my dad was surprised and angry, as it turned out she had purposefully stopped taking the pills behind his back so that she could drink.

An old MacLean's article from 1949 said this about Antabuse:

"Antabuse does nothing at all to remove whatever may be the cause of an alcoholic's craving. It merely helps him, through fear of the consequences of drinking while he is using it, to leave the stuff strictly alone."[10]

Because I remembered Antabuse from my childhood I went to my physician's office in my early thirties to ask for a prescription for myself, just as my mother had. I remember the shame I felt when I picked up the prescription from the

---

[10] Peter Davidson, *"The Truth about Antabuse,"* Maclean's Magazine, October 1, 1949, accessed November 4, 2019
https://archive.macleans.ca/article/1949/10/1/the-truth-about-antabuse

pharmacy, knowing I would walk out of there with another confirmation of my alcoholism. I felt weak and I felt as if I were[11] a failure. I used the Antabuse a little to help me not drink. For example, if I knew I would be tempted, and I knew I had to work the next day, I would take a pill to help make sure I wouldn't pick up a drink. The known unpleasant side effects are helpful in dissuading alcoholics to drink. It did work a little bit for me, as there were a few occasions where if I had not known I had Antabuse in my system, I surely would have started drinking. It helped me follow through with my good intentions to not drink. All of us alcoholics, on far too many occasions, have succumbed to the Drink, despite good, honest intentions to stay away from it.

Waiting for the Liquor Store to Open

You would be surprised and saddened to see the number of people waiting in the morning for the liquor or beer store to open. I would assume that on the occasions when I myself arrived at the liquor store at the moment the store opened, most of others in the line were doing the same thing as me: fighting a craving, an obsession, and a compulsion to drink that was so incessant that nothing else mattered, not even the potential embarrassment of standing in a line waiting for the doors of the liquor store to be unlocked. I was that person. I was also that sad and pathetic person who walked into the same liquor store two days in a row wearing the same dress. It was the walk of shame, the walk of alcoholism. On that morning I had woken up with a need to get relief that was a little worse than usual. I must have slept a little longer than normal and I had an insatiable craving; I needed a drink quickly. I got up, and with no care about how I looked or what I was wearing, I got in my car, still wearing my clothes from the night before, and I drove right to the liquor store. I walked in and as I walked past the

---

[11] Omudhome Ogbru. *"Antabuse,"*
https://www.medicinenet.com/disulfiram-oral/article.htm,
accessed November 4, 2019.

checkout and into the aisle, I looked at the liquor store worker and recognized that he was the same guy who had cashed me out just 12 hours earlier. He looked at me with pity as I stood there. Only an alcoholic would be capable of standing there in yesterday's rumpled clothes. He knew my secret. He knew I was an alcoholic.

To me, this meant one more person knew. I can still see that dress in my mind today and I remember throwing it out because of the memory and feelings that had become associated with it. That dress represented alcoholism and it also told me that I had sunk to a new low. Each alcoholic comes to their personal low, as they spiral further down their own rabbit hole. The problem is, usually, we accept the new low because we see no other choice. It becomes a bit of a conundrum. We need relief and relief is The Drink. At least that's all we see or feel it to be. The Drink is killing us, but we need it. The Drink is the only way we see out of the pain and discomfort we are in.

My alcoholism progressed to the point where drinking meant making sure I had enough days off in a row, with no appointments, so that I could drink like I knew I was going to, to drink like I wanted to, and to drink like I had to. Once I picked up my booze I would drink non-stop for days and I came to accept the nights that were taken away from me, in terms of both time and memory, forever dissolved into the cloud of alcoholism. The insane part of this dire situation is that it takes a near-death event or divine intervention to get an alcoholic to put down The Drink. We continue to try anything and everything we can think of to not have to stop drinking. We do this because, at this point, alcohol is both our relief kit and our best friend. Endless and total effort, and sometimes years and decades, are put into this attempt to continue to drink. To continue to drink is all that matters and most alcoholics continue to drink at all costs. When we boil this down and concentrate on what drinking ends up meaning to the end-stage alcoholic, it is this: to keep drinking means to have a best friend (alcohol) and to get relief (coping mechanism). How could a person in the midst of such a desperate state let go of their relief and their best friend at the same time? If you were to honestly ask yourself right now who your best friend is, and also where you get your relief from when you need it, what would your answer be? Now, imagine cutting both of them out of your life at the same time … while, I might add, deep in the bottom of a dark, dreadful hole. It's almost impossible. I hope that gives you a glimpse into understanding what it's like for an alcoholic in the midst of their ongoing battle to even entertain thoughts of giving up drinking. It is unfathomable. It is for this exact reason that I, like so many others, continued to reach for the Drink—my relief and my best friend—because I just didn't know of any way out of the corner I felt I was in. I am reminded of a statement by the author of the novel *Blackout* that really resonated with me. "Alcohol is not a cure for the pain, it is merely a postponement."[12] I wish I could determine who originated a description I once heard about the craving to drink so I could credit the brilliance of the author who wrote it. I believe it was either Caroline Knapp (who wrote *Drinking, A Love Story*) or Sarah Hepola (who wrote *Blackout*). With sincere apologies for being unable to properly attribute the phrase, I will paraphrase it here: "When your craving to drink is peaking, your pain is floating so high on the surface of your awareness it is like a lily pad at the surface of a pond. It is in your face and you can't get away from it. You have no choice but to postpone the pain and the only way to do that is to take a drink." That is exactly what a craving was like for me. And so I continued to drink.

The Drinking and Withdrawal Cycle

In the last years of my drinking, I suffered through many nights of terrible withdrawals. Withdrawals are like getting yourself ripped apart from the inside. You feel your nervous

---

[12] Hepola, Sarah, Blackout, *Remembering the Things I Drank to Forget,* Grand Central Publishing, 2016. Page 184

system viscerally in overdrive as you try desperately to restore balance after days of hard-drinking. Your body feels so rigid that you fear that a nervous twitch or pre-seizing shiver will make your brittle bones snap. While this is going on in the physical body, your mind is simultaneously screaming for another drink.

Once, when I was trying to stop drinking after a binge, I attempted to detox and go through the agonies of withdrawal on my own at home. Detoxing for the alcoholic is not like a juice cleanse at all, it can be more likened to human torture. Because the body has become so dependent on alcohol, the body and nervous system go into a form of shock once you stop drinking. Mild cases of withdrawal can be managed with fluids and pain relief for the headache you get, but in severe cases medications are required to prevent alcohol withdrawal seizures. On this particular occasion, I had no Valium or Ativan on hand to help me manage the withdrawals. Ativan and Valium are both benzodiazepines which are a class of prescription drugs used to treat anxiety and alcohol withdrawal. Even though I was desperately trying not to drink again that day, without the help of a benzodiazepine I just couldn't handle it and I succumbed. I called a friend who I knew would show up with a bottle of wine.

He arrived at my door. I took a couple of sips of the wine he had brought. Then a minute or two later I took another. Normally I would feel instant relief; this was different. I felt as if I were trying to survive, and a numbing dizziness came over me, along with a rigid sensation in my jaw. It felt heavy, more pronounced, as if it had morphed into a much larger appendage that was now protruding from my face. That is the last thing I remember before my friend saw me go into what's called a tonic-clonic alcohol withdrawal seizure. He shook me and this roused me out of it. After the seizure, I felt groggy and tired, yet I was unable to sleep. My nervous system was not able to recalibrate after the days, weeks, months and years of abuse

I had inflicted on it through my excessive drinking. My mind was racing and my physical body was so tightly wound up it was almost unbearable. About an hour later I noticed a hint of the same odd feelings around my jaw that had precipitated the seizure I had had just an hour or so earlier. I was worried that I might have another seizure and I panicked. It was such a scary time, as I could no longer control what was happening to my body.

I had my friend drive me immediately to the Emergency Room (ER) and while I was being helped through the lobby of my building and into the car, I barely had the use of my legs. They felt extra-long and thin, like pieces of spaghetti, and I was afraid of walking too slowly in case they buckled under me. I needed the momentum of a fast pace to keep me upright. I was assessed by the same Emergency Room (ER) doctor with whom I had worked with just one week earlier and I was worried that he—or someone else in the hospital—would recognize me. I don't think he did, although if he did he didn't say anything. It may seem strange that I would take myself to the same ER that I worked at, but as I mentioned earlier, at this stage of my alcoholism, I couldn't hold down a regular job so I worked for a nursing agency in Toronto. This allowed me to schedule myself on a day-to-day basis and it was perfect for an alcoholic binge drinker. The St. Joseph's ER where I had worked had been short-staffed for the previous few months so when I made myself available I would often end up being booked to work there. The reason that I went to that same ER as a patient in the throes of withdrawal is because I was desperate and scared, and it was the closest hospital to me. When you need medical help for alcohol withdrawal management, you are in desperate crisis mode and nothing else matters. Not the shame of your behaviour, or the potential embarrassment of being recognized and identified as an alcoholic.

After being hydrated and medicated to prevent seizures, I was sent on my way, with a prescription for Valium, to complete my withdrawal at home. I learned that evening that I could never again safely withdraw from using alcohol without medical management.

My drinking and withdrawal cycle was doomed to repeat itself. About a month later I was again taken to the St. Joseph's Hospital Emergency Room (ER) in need of another detox and some withdrawal care and medication. This time, the nurse assigned to take care of me recognized me immediately. I had just two weeks earlier been buddied with her to work in the Crisis Centre. At St. Joseph's Hospital, the Crisis Centre is the area of the ER that deals entirely with addictions, specifically alcohol and drug withdrawals. All ER nurses rotate through the Crisis Centre, and I got the feeling, while working there, that nobody is really keen on that post. So there I was, a full-blown alcoholic being treated for alcohol withdrawal when just weeks earlier I had been on the other side of things, in the exact same unit, caring for people in exactly my situation. My experience working with this nurse in the Crisis Centre had not been a good one. I remember that shift vividly, as this particular nurse was only in her late-twenties, and yet she was obese to the point where it interfered with her breathing, even with minimal exertion. She was short of breath and had to dab the sweat that accumulated on her brow so often that she carried a hankie in her hand. It was a bit of a sad picture, as she obviously had an eating disorder, but the irony of the situation was, in some respects, we weren't all that different; she was eating her pain away and I was drinking my pain away.

The worst part of working with this nurse had been she had a subtle sense of disdain towards the patients and even went as far as making a derogatory comment about one of them. I remember wanting to speak up in defense of him, and the Disease we both shared. He had no more chosen to be where he was in life than this young obese nurse had "chosen" her obesity. I felt there was not much difference between me as an alcoholic and the obese nurse I worked with. Obese Nurse and

Alcoholic Nurse. We were each eating or drinking through a deep underlying source of pain. Recovery was equally needed in both situations. When I found myself being cared for by the obese nurse, I remember saying to her, "I am not a bad person" … like I felt I needed to defend my character, which was truly how I felt.

The Gambling Continued

This cycle of binge drinking, detox, get back to work, drink, detox, get back to work, went on for a couple of years. I remained in the Russian Roulette phase of my Alcoholism, but the stakes became higher. There were multiple trips to detox and emergency rooms, and I began to be increasingly susceptible to alcohol withdrawal seizures. I lost my driver's license because any person who comes into the ER for any kind of seizure must by law have their license revoked pending further investigation. Despite all of the ramifications, I continued to drink.

I called in sick repeatedly to work while drunk, and I spent days alone in isolation so I could drink. I rarely ate anything or engaged in self-care of any kind and I began to wake up early in the morning shaking violently, desperate for a drink. I repeatedly administered to myself the necessary home withdrawal treatment I needed thanks to repeated prescriptions for benzodiazepines. I now knew full well that withdrawal seizures were bound to happen to me so I kept the benzos on hand. I don't mean to sound blasé about this. It is disturbing to me now to see how practical I had become about managing my addiction. I was at the point where I could not drink without ensuring I had medications on hand so I could detox myself, or I knew I would be again in the ER for treatment for withdrawal. I know this sounds crazy and trust me when I say I knew it would have been far better to simply stop drinking. I just couldn't do it. At this point in my life, I lived next door to a grocery market and in my final days of drinking I would run into this little store at all hours—while drunk and in blackouts—to get supplies such as cigarettes and juice. Sometimes I would only know that I had been there when I woke up the next morning to find evidence that I had stumbled home with new purchases. After a particularly long stretch of binge drinking, one that lasted longer than a week, I went into this store sober during the day. After the cashier rang in my purchase, she looked me in the eye and said, "I am praying for you."

I knew instantly where this was coming from. That was a painfully powerful moment for me and each time I think of it my eyes still well up with tears. That lady in the grocery store touched something deep inside me that day when she said she was praying for me. That was a powerful spiritual experience for me, and I think it was about one soul connecting and communicating with another. I was a very sad and desperate woman; I needed any prayer I could get, and she knew it.

Despite all of these abnormal, painful, humiliating, and tragic experiences, I was powerless to stop drinking. I drank whenever I could. I was tempting death, either through life-threatening withdrawal symptoms or through self-inflicted harm. I continued dancing with the devil and with death, dipping my toes back into the hot flames in the deep dark well I would move towards each time I lost myself. I was now going to such a dark, disconnected place while drinking that I began to attempt to kill myself while in blackouts. One attempt occurred when I swallowed the entire contents of two full, newly-dispensed bottles of pills, one of which contained Ativan; the other held something called Imovane, a type of sedative, or, in layman's terms, sleeping pills. I later found out that I had called my brother drunk and told him what I was going to do. I passed out with no recollection of the call. By the grace of God, I woke up with my brain intact, two empty pill bottles, and a big Imovane-blue and Ativan-riddled puddle of vomit bedside me. I have no memory of any of these suicide attempts, as I was drunk and in a blackout. Each time, by the grace of God, I escaped harm. I remember nothing. Thank You, God.

The Same Path My Mother Had Taken

So here I was sliding rapidly down the same treacherous path my mother had blazed before me. I was becoming the one person I had vowed I would not become, and living out the exact undesirable ending. I was living the alcoholic's worst nightmare, which is to die a slow, painful, and lonely alcoholic death. Alcoholism is a very desolate disease and at the end phase of their drinking, many alcoholics find themselves alone and isolated. That's what happened to my mother, who succeeding in drinking herself to death in 2009. One year later, in 2010, my drinking had progressed to the point where I, too, was in the lonely end phase; friends and family had stopped calling, mostly because I had burned them out. There I was going down the same tragic alcoholic path as my mother— her death still fresh in everyone's minds, including mine. I was terrified and I felt so alone. How I wished somebody could have reached out and helped me. But the thing is, I never reached out to anyone, either. I remember overhearing one of my family members saying, "She's just like her mother." It was now not even a secret that I was an alcoholic; it was merely an accepted fact. I don't believe anyone around me had the capacity to help me in any way, and nobody did. The two people closest to me were my brother and a dear long-time girlfriend. They were friends themselves, and both knew I was spinning out of control and dying inside. They stopped calling me or including me in anything, which was my fault entirely. I know that they both loved and cared for me, and oh how I wish there had been an intervention. But for a long time, the Mrs. Hyde part of me had been pushing them away, and the truth is, this angry, obnoxious addict may not have been able to accept it anyway. Addiction is so very complicated. So for those reading, if your olive branch is being rejected, allow the rejection, take care of yourself, and don't underestimate the power of positive thoughts. Pray for them.

I think that one of the hardest parts at the end stage of any alcoholic's path is the isolation we create for ourselves. My own isolation distorted my perception and scrambled my thinking; it seemed like my brother and my friend just sat by silently while I destroyed more of my life and my health. I felt hurt like I had been written off. I think part of what made this situation so difficult, at least in my brother's case, was that while growing up he himself had not received or experienced what proper healthy relationships looked and felt like and he himself was broken, so he did not know how to be in one with me. He needed love and support himself; there was nothing extra available to give to me. Once I got sober I felt resentful and angry. Hadn't anybody loved me enough to fight for me? If there is an alcoholic in your life, I invite you to make an effort to intervene in the self-destructive behaviour that will surely end in their death if they don't get help. At the very least your action will serve to plant a seed that might ultimately flower into hope. Please don't write them off. Yes, they may be rude, obnoxious, selfish and mean. Their behaviour may be self-destructive and embarrassing, as well. I assure you they are also hurting and lost, and they can't find their way home to who they truly are. They need your help.

It takes an enormous amount of courage and compassion to confront an alcoholic and dare them to look after the precious life they have been given. I know I became a painful burden and my behaviour was, at times, very difficult to deal with. I never intended things to be that way. And I didn't desire it. Alcoholics are poor judges of their own behaviour and, looking back, I would have given anything to have had someone in my life who cared about me, someone who could deliver the tough love messages that might have shown that I was loved, worthy and valued. I should make it clear that I am not *negating* or diminishing any of my behaviours, and I know at times I was not the easiest person to be around. I am truly sorry to have been so troubling. Honestly, it was the last thing I ever wanted because my own mother had put both me and my brothers through the exact same misery. My older brother came to help me once after I had made a drunken plea to him for help over the telephone. It was right before I entered treatment and I was in a bad state. I am not sure what I said on that drunken call but when I heard his knock at my door I remember feeling so glad that he was willing to take time out of his workday to visit me. But then I instantly realized what he was walking into. There I was, lying on my couch drunk, disheveled, and unkempt, and with bottles and trash surrounding me. This was possibly a worse state than my brother had ever found our mother in and it's one of my most emotionally painful memories. I know he, like me, has deep grooves of pain in him that were caused by our mother's behaviour and I did more than open the wound that day. Sorry, Mike. He cleaned for an hour, and then went to the store, got me something to eat, and bought some supplies to help take care of me. I remember the nervous misery radiating off him as he said goodbye. I was embarrassed, humiliated and ashamed, but underneath it all, I was hurting and lonely. I drank again after he left and that night I tried to kill myself while in a blackout.

Years of Healing and Therapy

Through years of healing and therapy, I have come to understand that every person's behaviour has a story. Our behaviour and how we react in difficult situations are driven by our past sorrows and previous losses. We have all been shaped by our painful experiences. As I write, I think of the lyrics to the beautiful Madonna song "Oh Father," where she expresses what it was like getting used to the hurt and pain of her childhood. To summarize a few of my favorite lines in this song, it seemed to me she was saying this: "Maybe one day, when I look back, I will see that somebody hurt you, too." It is with this knowledge and insight that I try to harbour no anger towards anyone, and I am increasingly able to have compassion for how poorly-equipped I and all of my loved ones were to cope with my addiction. They were the products of their environments, too. Including my mother and father. While writing this book, I struggled with the emotions brought up by the behaviour of some of my friends during this period and after, and it's been a good reminder to feel compassion; they, too, have been hurt and carry sorrows.

Shortly before my mother died from alcoholism in 2009 she had witnessed enough of my drinking to know I was going down the same tragic path that she had travelled. On one occasion I had actually been drinking with my mother for a few days. To say that it was not a good time for either of us is an understatement. When I think back, I feel sadness and disgrace. I felt these emotions for both of us independently but also collectively as a mother and daughter repeating an unhealthy cycle. There is a profound sadness involved in being a witness to and a participant in this kind of tragedy. On this particular evening I had been binge drinking for six days straight. I was at the point where I was feeling too sick to continue drinking but even though I wanted to and needed to quit, it just wasn't that simple. I needed help to manage the effects of alcohol withdrawal. My mom gave me a dose of Ativan to help put me to sleep and to prevent seizures while coming down and out of the stupor I was in. I will never forget what she said to me as she walked out of the bathroom that day: "You know, Tina … it gets worse." That was all she had for me. The day my mother said that to me I felt a sense of impending doom, as though I had no bargaining resources left. Nobody around me had the capacity to help me, nor were they equipped with any tools to support me in any way.

You know, Tina, it gets worse.

You know, Tina, it gets worse.

You know, Tina, it gets worse.

I will never forget the moment when I heard my mother say that to me. I knew on so many levels what that meant. It meant the Disease was powerful, and my mother knew it. She couldn't help herself, and how could she possibly even begin to help me? The sad part was that I knew these words to be true when she said them and I felt the doom to my core. I think my mom did help me that day, because not only did that statement never leave me, but it was a moment of truth so powerful it gave me clarity of what truly lay ahead for me.

This picture basically captures the bottoming out of my life and the end of my drinking days. Hitting bottom in my drinking journey actually played out over a long, slow, and painful period. Mine was no epic story. There was no added catastrophic event that led me to quit. There was no abrupt end to my drinking career; it was more like the slow peeling off of a band-aid. Some people's bottoms happen as a result of a major tragic event i.e. they are charged with impaired driving, fired from their job, lose their marriage, or even charged with a criminal offense and incarcerated. My bottom was a repeated crashing in and around the same low place I'd been hovering for years, constantly feeling the pull of the undertow that threatened to ultimately drown me in Drink.

My journey to end my drinking was classic, textbook AA. It was one alcoholic talking to another. What happened for me was this: I had a visit from a friend who had not only been my realtor in the past, but also an occasional drinking buddy. This friend was witness to the tragic spiral of my mother's life, as he had become her realtor when she returned to Canada two years earlier. He knew of her recent passing and judging by the drunken state I was in, he could see the writing on the wall. I remember the concerned look on his face and I could feel that he was worried for my life.

He gave me the name and number of a friend of his who was in Alcoholics Anonymous (AA), and he told me to give him a call. Despite the fact that I was weary and sick from how badly the Disease had taken hold of me, I pushed my friend's concerns aside and continued drinking myself into oblivion again that night. But the Universe was at play here and not long after my realtor friend gave me the number of the guy in AA, I found myself once again in such a desperate state that I called the guy. The man's name was Luc and he suggested we meet on Lakeshore Boulevard near where we both lived. I had already shared I was drinking a lot and might need help. I told him straight up, I was drinking and I was going to bring a drink with me. He understood, met me, and we talked some more. And this is when the magic started to happen, just like the AA Big Book says, one alcoholic to another. It felt refreshing to say aloud to another human being—who was an alcoholic just like me—the truths about my drinking and to realize I was not alone. This man picked me up and took me to my first meeting of Alcoholics Anonymous. One conversation with another alcoholic, paired with one meeting, and I was ready to throw in the towel on trying to drink like a normal person. Now, I know it sounds incredible that after such a short time I would be ready to give up all I had been holding onto, but in truth the feeling of hope I gained from my brief interaction with AA, and its people, was powerful, and it carried a lot of weight. It was the beacon of light I had been so desperately seeking.

This gentleman helped me immensely during my first few months of trying to stay sober. I will be forever grateful to him and to the AA program. Sadly, I must write that my friend Luc tragically ended his own life just four weeks before I began to write this book. Not everyone makes it, and all any of us get is a daily reprieve.

The Questions to Ask Yourself:
Am I in a circumstance at this moment that I'd like to change? If yes, can I take one step or make one decision that will support this change, knowing the Universe will join me?

7

Living Sober—Rehab

Although I'm not actively drinking, I live every day with the Disease dormant in me, like the chickenpox lives in those of us who have had it. The Disease not only lives there, but it is subliminally, and on deep cellular levels, poking at me all the time. I make a choice to live a sober life every minute of every day in order to make sure I don't slide back into the pit of hell I lived in before I got myself into a recovery program. I feel I need to stand on guard against what I consider to be the cunning nature of the Disease of alcoholism—of any addiction, really. I understand why people who are not alcoholics don't take this issue as seriously as those of us whose lives have teetered on the brink of personal annihilation. Statistics show an estimated seven percent[13] of Americans currently meet the criteria for alcoholism and it's estimated 18% of Canadians meet that criteria at some point in their lives.[14] By contrast, one in two people is likely to get cancer and one in four is likely to die from it.[15] Alcoholism doesn't have the visibility in our national health care systems or in our news reports that cancer has. And yet in North America, alcohol consumption is the third-leading cause of preventable death, after cancer and heart disease.[16]

To get a sense of how pernicious this horrible Disease is we need to look no further than the lives of many actors and musicians who struggled for years before succumbing to an alcohol-related death. Take actor Philip Seymour Hoffman, for

---

[13] Abuse and Treatment Statistics in the US, Project Know, *https://www.projectknow.com/drug-addiction/statistics/*

[14] Substance Use and Addiction, Canadian Mental Health Association https://ontario.cmha.ca/addiction-and-substance-misuse/

[15] Cancer Statistics at a Glance, Canadian Cancer Society, https://www.cancer.ca/en/cancer-information/cancer-101/cancer-statistics-at-a-glance/?region=on

[16] Abuse and Treatment Statistics in the US, Project Know, https://www.projectknow.com/drug-addiction/statistics/

example. His story stops me in my tracks and fills me with sorrow, sadness, and fear. Here's a man who started drinking casually in 2014, after two decades of sobriety. He soon added opioids to his playlist and then he started using heroin. Within months he was dead of an overdose. His death was a tragedy. He had lived an exemplary life of recovery ... until he didn't. Hoffman's longtime partner, Mimi O'Donnell, wrote movingly of the experience of walking beside him as he travelled down the path of relapse.

"The addiction is always lurking just below the surface looking for a moment of weakness to come roaring back to life,"[17] she wrote. I can attest that my own experiences support the accuracy of this description, and I have done my best to narrate my first-hand experiences with the lurking. I admire the courage Mimi O'Donnell displayed to so honestly share her experience, knowledge, and understanding of addictions. She has helped shed light on the topic and dispel the myths around one of the most misunderstood aspects of addiction and overdose. Which is this: it is not just *one* event or *one* reaction to just *one* singular life event that leads to relapse. It is much more complicated than that. Even people who are doing well with their sobriety will still at times feel they are engaged in a battle to the death and I think this will always be so.

I suspect it can be hard for people who don't have this disease lying dormant within them to understand just how vigilant we alcoholics must be in order to keep body and soul together. And some people may think I'm exaggerating the situation, or being overly dramatic, or even just a little bit uptight. You may be thinking that triumphing over alcoholism is just a question of putting mind over matter. That we alcoholics should just toughen up, show more strength, or get our act together. You might further be thinking, we're doing this to ourselves. That,

---

[17] Mimi O'Donnell, "Mimi O'Donnell Reflects on the Loss of Philip Seymour Hoffman and the Devastation of Addiction," Vogue Magazine, December 13, 2017, accessed November 4, 2019

if we really cared about our friends and families, we wouldn't put them through the misery of our "shameful and immoral behaviour." That somehow we are *choosing* to drink so much that we run ourselves to the edge of death.

God knows I wish it were that easy.

I have learned alcoholism is like a gaseous home invader who sneaks in through an unlocked window while you are asleep and takes up residence in the furnace in the basement, ready to infiltrate every corner of the house and poison you when you least expect it to attack. You can't see it, you can't smell it and you can't hear it. But it's there all the time, waiting for you to turn up the heat so it can fill your lungs with the poison of addiction and seduce you into taking one drink, and then another, and another, until you are, like Phillip Seymour Hoffman and so many others like him, trapped, powerless, and, ultimately, dead.

For those of us who consider ourselves alcoholics, The Drink is not a choice we make. It is an entity that is planning our execution. An unknown author has penned a poem that beautifully sums up what we're up against:

I Am Your Disease

I am Your Disease.

I hate meetings.
I hate your higher power.
I hate anyone who has a program.

To all who come in contact with me,
I wish you suffering and death.

Allow me to introduce myself …
I am the disease of addiction.

Alcoholism, drugs and eating disorders.
I am cunning, baffling and powerful. That's me!

I've killed millions and enjoyed doing it.

I love to catch you by surprise.
I love pretending I'm your friend and lover.

I've given you comfort.
Wasn't I there when you were lonely?

When you wanted to die, didn't you call on me?

I love to make you hurt.
I love to make you cry. Better yet …
I love it when I make you so numb,
You can't hurt and you can't cry.
You feel nothing at all.

I give you instant gratification.
All I ask for in return is long term suffering.
I've always been there for you.

When things were going right, you invited me back.
You said you didn't deserve to be happy.
I agreed with you.
Together we were able to destroy your life.

People don't take me seriously.
They take strokes seriously.
They take heart attacks seriously.
Even diabetes, they take seriously.
Yet, without my help, these things wouldn't be possible.

I'm such a hated disease, yet I don't come uninvited.
You choose to have me.
Many have chosen me, instead of love and peace.

I hate all of you who work a 12-step program.
Your program, your meetings, and your higher power weaken me.
I can't function in the manner I am accustomed to.

I am your disease.
For now I must lie here quietly.
You don't see me, but I'm growing more powerful every day.

When you settle for mere existence, I thrive.

When you feel fully alive, I weaken.
But I'm always here waiting for you.

Until we meet again,
I wish you continued suffering and death.
  –Author Unknown

I initially tried to quit drinking by attending AA meetings and by doing the work suggested in the program of Alcoholics Anonymous. I had a sponsor. I did service and I started to work my way through the Twelve Steps, including prayer. All of my efforts together were no match for the challenges of living sober and suddenly wide awake in the world and feeling everything. Because I had been living in a numbed state for so long, there was a fresh intensity to all that I was feeling.

In the very beginning, there was a great sense of relief in coming out to the world and admit that I was indeed an alcoholic. There was no more lying, hiding drunk, and living the secret dual life of a drunk and a nurse. I felt the burden of keeping my secret, lift, as though an immense weight were lifted from me. I really loved being in truth and I think this was the point at which I began my quest for truthful living.

In the very beginning of my commitment to sobriety, I experienced a slight phase of euphoria, but it did not last long for me. People in recovery call this euphoric phase a "pink cloud" to describe the feelings of elation and happiness that show up, but I look at it as a combination of things. One of them is the realization that there really is a way to live life without the Drink, and it is very freeing. Another arises from the recognition you have avoided disaster and escaped death. And quite possibly the most important factor, at least for me, was I began to learn and even feel energetically there was something in this life that was higher than myself, and it's with me at all times. This "something that is higher" gives order, meaning, and purpose to my life. For many, this understanding marks the very beginning of their relationship with their higher power, and that was the case for me.

My first period of sobriety lasted from mid-January 2011 to the end of June. I had been doing pretty well for the first few months, keeping very busy with regular shifts at the hospital and going to AA meetings. I had a sponsor, contributed service to my AA community, ate well, exercised, prayed and did yoga. I was trying hard to take care of myself and do the work set out by the AA program, but I was struggling to manage all that I was feeling. Yes, I needed relief, but I was also feeling the weight of what felt like a lifetime of lost years and so much wasted time. I felt a matrix of emotions ranging from hurt, shame, fear and anger to regret. I couldn't cope without The Drink and I desperately needed a reprieve. Despite my efforts, the discomfort I was feeling was too much for me to handle and I relapsed.

And if I hadn't believed or understood this was a progressive disease before, I sure did now, because it was a relapse of epic proportions. I proceeded to go on a seven-or-eight-day bender that was the worst one yet. At the end of this drinking binge, while in a blackout I called my friend Kelly and told her I was going to jump off of my 33-story building. I do recall going up to the 33rd floor while drinking to have a look at my options. But that's it. My friend Kelly took charge of my welfare and helped check me into a 28-day program in Toronto at Renascent, an Addiction Rehab Treatment Centre. Kelly was an integral part in my recovery and she was instrumental in saving my life. A person like me, and so many others with the same struggles as I had, can want sobriety badly, but we can't do it alone. Kelly helped me so much by providing the love, support, and resources I was lacking. Almost anyone can be admitted to this rehab program if you meet the requirements but you are put on a waitlist or given a date that might be as long away as two weeks to a month.

Too Long to Wait

This does not seem like a long time for most people, but for an alcoholic, in the Russian Roulette phase of their drinking, it is far too long. If you choose to pay out of your own pocket rather than wait for a government-subsidized placement you can be admitted within a day or two. Kelly paid for me to enter the program herself and I was able to get in almost immediately. This may have saved my life, and it felt good to me in a way that was quite foreign. I don't think I knew that Kelly had to pay for my bed in the treatment centre until I saw her get her cheque book out while doing the intake process. I remember feeling uncomfortable that she was paying, but I also remember feeling a shred of worth, and at that moment I sure needed it. Somebody invested in me. Somebody saw I had worth. My experience in rehab went something like this:

Day 1: Anxious, scared, and physically withdrawing from alcohol, benzos, and sleeping pills. One word: Horrible.

Day 2: Feeling a little better physically but mentally only wanting to get the F%$K out of here. My mind tells me I don't belong here and I am better than this. Four words: No I am not.

Day 3: One word. Brutal is all I can say. I want out and feel that I am wasting my time and my life is passing me by. Rules, rules, rules, cleaning toilets and eating shit food. My mind is a flurry of thoughts and most are about leaving. I'm thinking of how much I will miss during my 28-day stint, how bad I had to have screwed up to land my ass in here, but already forgetting my life was hanging on the line and it was primarily a drunk suicide attempt that precipitated my treatment.

And so the days passed. If it had not been for Kelly actually paying for me to be there in the first place, I would have most certainly bailed at that point. I felt a high level of accountability to follow through with something others had invested and I didn't want to let her down. I am so grateful that somewhere along the line of my upbringing I had learned accountability. For an alcoholic or addict to make it out of the depths of this disease, this quality of character is a must. I managed to make it through those awful first few days and then I settled in and resigned myself to the full 28 days of the program.

My brother visited me while I was in Rehab, and when I thanked him for coming he said, "Of course I came, you are my sister." The tone with which my brother delivered these words intimated he was there to support me through this, and to be there for me. The fantasy that the strong bond that my brother and I had could continue to pull me through in times of distress never faltered during my initial recovery process. The thing is, I was imagining things. Substance abuse had been part of our bond and part of how we had always connected in the past. In reality, there was no possibility of a relationship between us when I was sober and he was not. He did try to be a supportive brother; he showed up physically and he had some ideas around how he could be supportive. I'm guessing almost all recovering addicts hope their relationships with family members will evolve in a positive, nurturing way, but it usually does not happen that way. There is one really scary and challenging thing we need to understand, and that is the people we had relationships with when we were using may not know how to be with us when we are clean and sober, and they may unintentionally act in ways that function as triggers for relapse, as was my experience with my brother and my father. It was difficult for me, but I found it very important not to blame them, and to realize that they were probably still suffering with their own issues or, as might also be the case, there was a clash between two different, inconsistent, ways of life.

Honesty and Truth

Many people in recovery live out a value system that is strong in honesty and truth, and this is very scary for some people. I was relentlessly committed to my truth because it felt right and it helped me stay sober. But, sadly, I learned it was off-putting for some people. I definitely had a part in this, as I was probably too harsh about speaking my truth and in expecting too much from others. Over time it became clear to me that I had to figure out what was good for me, and what expectations were reasonable to impose upon others.

When it came to my family members, the gap between how I wanted to live my life now, and how I would need to be in order to continue my relationships with them, was too large. I didn't feel like there was a way for this sober version of Tina to co-exist with them. I would imagine that, if asked, they would strongly disagree with the idea that they couldn't have a relationship with me because I don't think they would be able to understand the ways that they themselves may have unknowingly acted as a trigger for me to drink. What's more, I'm not sure they fully comprehended the importance to me of honouring how I was now living. I learned that because I had been an addict for the majority of my life, I couldn't expect my family members or friends to suddenly turn the page and go forward with me without blinking an eye. They weren't willing to let me off the hook, nor were they willing to reflect on any contribution they may have made to my unwitting path towards alcoholism. At first, I felt they had wronged me. But I've come to realize this is my journey and that in the circumstances of my sobriety and my healing journey, we were simply no longer a healthy fit. I wish them healing and comfort.

As a result of my commitment to sobriety, the course of many relationships came to an end for me, one by one, throughout the first few years of my growth and evolution. Some relationships became a poor fit and I grew apart from some people. It was painful, yes, but the end of those relationships was the right outcome, as it was part of the evolution and growth of everyone involved. The truth is some relationships do run their course. They do end. And that is okay. I am still growing and evolving and the relationships in my life continue to shift and change along with me.

The LiveWell Recipe

While I was in treatment, I had the life-saving realization that if I wanted to remain sober I had to make important changes, and engage in a high level of self-care. My daily routine for staying sober was now evolving into what I now call my LiveWell Recipe. I added Psychotherapy into my Recipe, which would prove to be invaluable. The relapse I had experienced was a direct result of not being able to manage and control my feelings, emotions, and discomfort. Once I left the treatment centre I immediately began twice-weekly sessions with a clinical psychologist. This psychotherapy work has helped me on my journey of healing and the wondrously transformative process it invites. It has helped me to access the strength and courage to face myself fully and begin to reshape myself into the best version of myself that I can be. My therapist is a brilliant, compassionate, caring woman and I am blessed to still work with her today.

So, what was my LiveWell Recipe shaping into? It meant I was:

❖ Attending AA Meetings / Twelve-Step work
❖ Participating in psychotherapy
❖ Praying, and I ultimately began building a spiritual program
❖ Practicing yoga
❖ Trying to meditate
❖ Removing toxic people, places and things
❖ Making an effort to take responsibility for myself
❖ Committed to truthful living
❖ Developing a program of self-care

The result was that I was not drinking. The work had now begun, but it's important to realize the work never stops.

It is an understatement to say that after living most of one's life as an addict or alcoholic it's very difficult to suddenly start living sober. It takes time for your body, mind, heart, and soul to adjust to a radically different way of being in the world, and to learn a new set of behaviours that will support you in living sober for the first time—for many of us—since childhood. That is part of why the relapse rate is so high. I had two relapses, during the first 10 months of sobriety and both led me close to death. After my first relapse, I told my sponsor I was working with a therapist. She told me I could not do both, and I had to choose. I could either work with her or I could work with my therapist. When I asked her why I could not work with both, she said: "Well, then we wouldn't know what helped you."

I was flabbergasted! I was, scared shitless. I had just gotten out of rehab and, honestly, I did not care what was going to help me. I just knew I desperately wanted to live. Although vulnerable and new in the program I sensed that something was not right about this ultimatum. I ignored it, and I chose to work with both my therapist and the sponsor who had given me the ultimatum. I did not bring up the idea of therapy with my sponsor again and she just assumed I had chosen her. I share this only because had it not been for my clinical psychologist, I might not have made it through the tough times of my first year of sobriety and I might not be sober or even alive today.

A sponsor is someone who has been successfully working the Twelve Step program themselves, and their primary responsibility is to help a recovering alcoholic or addict work the Twelve Steps by providing explanation, guidance, and encouragement. Sponsorship is a basic part of belonging to a Twelve Step Fellowship and potentially one of its richest experiences. Although our sponsors often become our friends, this is not recommended as it does make it more difficult for them to provide the tough feedback that may be required to help keep a sponsee on track and sober.

My Experience

In my experience, I feel that to optimize success in sobriety it is beneficial for a person to work with their sponsor and a clinical psychologist or counselor at the same time. Sponsors are intended to support and guide members of the program, to take them through the AA book and to work the process of the

Twelve Steps. Sponsors are not supposed to give advice, veto a physician's directions, or tell a newly-sober person what they should or should not do with regards to medications, psychiatry or psychotherapy. Sometimes, the role of the sponsor can become more inflated than intended, and, on occasion there are some who start giving advice. At times I believe it is helpful to have an added source of support and guidance. It says in the Big Book that AA does not have all the answers. Psychiatrists and psychologists are important and necessary for many to maintain good mental health.

Sponsorship and Therapy

Myself and many others like me are confirmation of the idea that optimizing one's chances of getting sober and staying sober requires both sponsorship and therapy. The amazing 12-Step work done with sponsors unearths sources of pain and patterns of behaviour we begin to look at, and we also begin to see what our part has been in all that has happened to us. These are exactly the kind of issues that need further work with a professional therapist in a safe environment. We must also remember all sponsors in AA are members of AA themselves; they are alcoholics in recovery. Many of them are in no position to be giving advice to anyone. For example, when I parted ways with my first sponsor, I kindly expressed to her that I felt we were no longer a fit. I can't say what she was feeling, but my honest expression caused her to say this to me. "You need me." And it was said in a way that made me feel very uncomfortable, as though she wanted to make me change my mind.

If I hadn't been strong enough at that time, I might have believed her. I strongly feel there is a place for both sponsorship and psychotherapy in a recovery program, and that the percentage of success in sobriety increases when a person works with both.

I also believe it is intelligent to reach out for help in every direction available, and that it is optimal to do more than just the AA program, and add other elements to your recovery program, as I am suggesting in my LiveWell Recipe.

A Crucial Milestone

The one-year mark represents a crucial milestone in an alcoholic's recovery, and it is where some say the real work begins. I did not rest on my laurels, and to make sure I was safe, I put more effort into my LiveWell Recipe. You can want it, feel it, see it, know it, yearn for it, and need it … but the only way to have it is, do it! For me, once I started making changes and doing the work of building and implementing my LiveWell Recipe, I could feel a shift in the right direction and this helped me continue; in fact, it propelled me to want to do more.

The hard part in a recovery journey is there is no more numbing, no more shifting of the feelings and stirrings you feel inside. This creates new problems and struggles. If you are feeding a void inside of you with a drug, a substance, or an unhealthy behaviour of choice, and you remove it, then it's almost guaranteed, in time, something else will come up to take the place of your original addiction or coping modality—it's a form of "symptom substitution." In essence, the addiction or behaviour moves around from one area of your life to another; it shape-shifts because we feel compelled to use *something* to control and manage how we feel. Feel pain? Eat, drink, drug, work, engage with phone or laptop, etc. Feel hurt? Eat, drink, drug, work, engage with phone or laptop, etc. Feel anxious? Eat, drink, drug, work, engage with phone or laptop, etc. It becomes normal for us to use our chosen modality to shift how we feel. My work with my clinical psychologist helped me get to the source of my pain and bit by bit, layer by layer, process it and transmute it so it no longer had such a strong grip on my emotions or my behaviour. This is of utmost importance, as it is the pain itself that triggers the need to fill the void that led to the addiction or coping modality in the first place. I have personally experienced that, over time, and with continued therapy, the addiction component of my character or the void inside of me has decreased and softened. The impact this part of me has on my thought processing and decision making has become smaller and smaller as if the "reaction dial" has been turned down.

The ways the addictive component manifests itself—and the form into which it shifts once you have stopped practicing your primary addiction—varies in everyone. It may be as simple as increased snacking, or it might transform into a pattern of overworking or over-exercising, or a new gambling addiction or an eating disorder—or smoking, which might include cigarettes or marijuana. All of these behaviours continue to harbour the addictive part of the person. Some behaviours may be less harmful or more socially acceptable, but we must remember that they still exist. The bottom line here is we have not yet learned to be inside of ourselves, how to feel, and how to tolerate loneliness and pain. Work in progress.

Addictions Move Around Trembling

I was a perfect example of how addictions move around. The first leg of my journey to manage my addictions started with getting sober and eliminating alcohol and prescription pills. I quickly experienced the fact the addictive part of me needed to be appeased. With these modalities no longer available I relied on cigarettes and snack eating. After some time in recovery, living sober, and engaging in my LiveWell Recipe, I was able to dial down the intensity of the addictive part of me a small amount. After six months, I quit smoking. I had progressed in my psychotherapy to where I was now beginning to be able to rely on some new coping mechanisms and my own emotional strength. For a while, the only addictive traits or behaviours that were active in me were exercise and my snacking. I wasn't drinking, taking any pills or smoking. I was engaging with my LiveWell Recipe and making progress. But the discomfort still existed within me enough that at times I still felt like I needed more relief. I needed to move away from the discomfort, but I couldn't use alcohol, cigarettes or pills to help me do that. So, the addictive part of me prompted me to adopt a new behaviour in an attempt to appease the discomfort. I succumbed to an addiction issue called Bulimia Nervosa. Never before had eating disorders been a part of my story, but now I was eating a whole pint of Haagen-Dazs ice cream and then sticking my fingers down my throat to force myself to vomit. It is uncanny how the voice of alcoholism that was in my head for all those years showed up as the same voice of my new addiction, the eating disorder. The voice and the feelings associated with it felt familiar and comfortable, as would an old friend coming back into your life. But this was not a friend. Once again I was feeling silent, ashamed and isolated. I was not feeling good about myself, as you can imagine, as I was now carrying a new secret. It didn't feel right, and I knew deep down in the fabric of my being this was an unhealthy path to follow, especially since I realized it could lead me back to drinking. This meant the addictive part of me had to find another new, healthier way to manage the stirrings.

Essentially, it turned out that I had removed the addictive behaviours—drinking, smoking, and pills—faster than I had been able to work through the part of me that embraced addiction. This part of me was still very alive and powerful and I had not yet developed enough strategies to handle the addictive part of me that remained. Bulimia kept me from some perceptively worse addictions but I knew this was an unhealthy path, too, and I knew in my gut I had to be truthful about it or I would slide back to drinking. And back to drinking is exactly what would have eventually happened, as the slide back starts with stepping onto the slippery slope, and the Bulimia was the stepping-stone.

My wellness mantra was, "No stone unturned," so I shared this new dark secret with my therapist and then also with one of my girlfriends. The intent and power behind releasing this secret was to both live in my truth and to get off of the slope. From the day I unleashed that secret, I managed to not binge and purge again. The experience was part of learning my wellness is a work-in-progress and I will have to continually evolve and grow to manage my addictive tendencies; it's going to take a consistent focus on self-study and healing. I do know the addictive part of my personality and makeup is much smaller today than it has ever been. It does not control my life and with continued work, I expect this component of who I am will continue to become smaller and smaller and softer and softer. Today, I do no drinking, smoking, binging or purging but I do still rely on snacks, many, many snacks … ask my husband ☺. I am the Snack Queen.

Having gone through this difficult experience around becoming bulimic, I gained insight that led me to a better understanding of what so many of us struggle with as we attempt to live and manage our psychological makeup and unresolved feelings. Here is my simplified attempt to explain my experience with this process:

Trigger → Discomfort → Craving → Unhealthy Behaviour

The Unhealthy Behaviour is an elicited response from a chain of events that starts with a trigger.

Triggers can be social, environmental or emotional in nature, i.e. alcohol and food marketing campaigns, a painful memory, feelings of anger, or a number of fears.

Discomfort is an uncomfortable feeling or agitation. Craving is a powerful desire for something, or an urge.

I am one of many people who are feeding or filling a void inside of themselves with a number of modalities and behaviours, i.e. food, sex, gambling, drugs, checking text messages or emails, Facebook, etc. What we all have is a source of pain that gets triggered when the stirrings that accompany it are at the root of our addictive tendency or unhealthy behaviour. Have you ever heard anyone say someone was "eating their pain away" or doing some "stress eating"? I remember my first sponsor in early sobriety saying, "It's not The Drink that is your problem." And I thought, "this lady's crazy, that's my only problem." She went on to say, "It's the reason that you drink that is the problem. The source of the discomfort is the problem."

Is it Stirrings or Discomfort?

Is it Stirrings or is it Discomfort? My interpretation of Stirrings is this: brief, minor, flashes of uneasiness, restlessness, nervousness or anxiety. A brief and slight need to feel different that usually passes as quickly as it comes. The thing is, stirrings surface around thoughts all of the time and there is no getting away from them. There are millions of triggers behind them and we all experience them all day, every day. They are, however, closely linked to what I consider low level or low-grade discomfort. You could compare them to the feeling one gets before public speaking, or a concern over whether or not the bills will be paid, how you may feel when an old childhood memory surfaces, or when you're running late for work, or experiencing everyday stress around thoughts, etc. Some people seem to manage them and let them go, and there isn't a buildup where the stirrings turn into discomfort. Where others like me—an alcoholic—might experience the stirrings more intensely and experience these everyday stirrings as discomfort. So where some people easily manage stirrings and let them go, others are not able to manage as well and may end up on the path that leads to unhealthy behaviours. In the early days of my sobriety, I had a hard time managing these "stirrings" for a couple of reasons, one being that I believe I felt them especially intensely, as some of us do. The other reason this was difficult was that the only tool I had ever used to shift, change or move away from these stirrings had been to drink or drug. Initially, I struggled to find ways to cope and feel better before the stirrings I felt inside me could grow into discomfort. To live a sober life free of alcohol and feel *everything* was quite unsettling at first. So many feelings, memories, sadness, and pain flooded through my mind, leaving me with a lot of stirrings and discomfort I could no longer numb away, and my only recourse was to learn to work through them so they were less intense and more manageable. And so the work began.

By choosing to get sober, I felt like I had taken a big giant leap, like the Hindu deity Hanuman who jumped from Sri Lanka to India to save Citta, a damsel in distress. After I took the giant leap into sobriety, I felt like I was stretching far away from my old world and life. For some time, it was as if I were a new person who I didn't even know very well, and I was going through the motions of life. I just kept doing the next right thing, the next best thing, in each moment. I continued to build and adjust my LiveWell Recipe as I grew and evolved, adding new ingredients, or changing the amount of an existing ingredient. And, yes, I struggled at times, as every newly-sober person does. But I just kept at it, I kept doing the work in my recipe and I never gave up.

This LiveWell Recipe saved my life and over time it became my new design for living. Even on days when I would wake up gripped with fear and full of stirrings, the structure of my LiveWell Recipe guided me to start each day and get through each day. Not only did the ritualistic nature of my LiveWell Recipe help give order to any amount of chaos the day before me presented, but I also took comfort in the changeless order of it. Over time, I began to transform into a new, healthy version of myself. I let go of some parts of me and rebuilt others. I was beginning to feel the shift energetically and spiritually, as well. I started to relax a little as I polished my rough edges and moved out of survival mode. I had spent so much of my life in survival mode, it had become my norm, my default setting, but I no longer needed to be planted in it. This change was a little uncomfortable for me. It was like I was slowly peeling off layers and layers of armour I had pulled around me as a form of protection.

Congruent with my transformation, I noticed, as I shed those layers, a much gentler Tina began to show. My edges began to soften, along with my speech, my dress, my attitude and my reactions to my feelings. I have always resonated with the lotus flower because it symbolizes hope and comfort, and it gave me some confirmation that I was exactly where I should be. The lotus flower starts out stuck under the mud, deep down in the murky soil. Over time, it gains strength and sustenance to rise through and above the thick mud. Eventually blossoming and emerging as a beautiful flower. I liked to think of myself as a lotus flower. In my drinking days I was stuck deep in the mud and today I am a beautiful flower that rose above and through it all as Sober Tina.

I like to look at that time in my life as a waiting period, one in which I built up my mental and emotional strength. This is when I started to face all parts of myself. I learned to start viewing myself with compassion, love, and acceptance, and this allowed me to move closer to and get to know my intimate self. After I'd been sober a few months, many aspects of life began to improve and I started settling into my new design for living. I began to take charge of my life, take charge of how I was feeling, take responsibility for how I lived and how I felt. I stopped hoping and waiting for someone else to come and magically fix things. I simply started fixing things myself, bit by bit, and it worked.

Struggling with Discomfort, Change, and Shame

The challenging part was that no matter how hard I tried and no matter how hard I fought to do all the things in my LiveWell Recipe so I could stay sober, I still struggled with the discomfort of feeling everything. This is a very difficult phase of sobriety and most—if not all—addicts relapse at some point. The reason that relapse is part of recovery is because you are now living in the reality that requires you to endure all of what you are feeling. No numbing. Gone are the days when you can just drink or drug the feelings away. It's kind of like "restless leg syndrome," but it's more of a "restless I-am-now-sober syndrome."

This is not a time to rest and relax, it is a time to ramp up your LiveWell routine. It may mean you need to spend extra time engaging in self-care or any number of other things that are backed by the intent to feel better. Take charge, take responsibility and do more to feel better. It was during difficult times like this vulnerable phase that I learned it really was all up to me. I was the one who had to keep doing what was needed, to adhere to my LiveWell Recipe, so I would be okay, and manage to not pick up a drink. It was during this time, early on in sobriety when I realized how much of my life I had lived in a baseline state of discomfort.

AA provides an acronym that is meant to help prevent discomfort and relapse: HALT, short for Hungry, Angry, Lonely and Tired. The reason each of these states should be carefully considered is because each state is both a trigger and a discomfort. And they are all variables that should be, for the most part, within our control. Remember my previous explanation:

Trigger → Discomfort → Craving → Unhealthy Behaviour

Success, in preventing feelings of discomfort so you do not move forward in the chain of events above to the *Craving* phase, depends on keeping the HALT variables in check. It is all about eliminating or reducing triggers so you don't engage in unhealthy behaviours. I incorporated the practice of HALT into my life and I even upped the ante and added Cold to my list. I began to understand how each of these triggers had a direct impact on how I felt. I recognized, for the most part, these were variables I could control. And so that's where I put my focus. Today, I try to never get hungry, angry, lonely, tired or cold. I diligently carry snacks so I don't get hungry, I stay connected to people so I don't start feeling lonely, I try to make sure I get lots of rest so I am not tired, I always carry a sweater or scarf so I don't get cold, and, when I am angry, I remember to tell myself my anger is a sign something in my life at this moment needs some attention, and I check in with what that might be.

The Disease Begins to Talk

Early sobriety is no walk in the park, and after a few months of solid sobriety, thoughts of drinking started to creep in. I recognized I needed to be exceedingly truthful about my drinking-related thoughts and it was dangerous to keep any thoughts of drinking to myself.

In fact, it is extremely dangerous for any alcoholic to sit alone with drinking-related thoughts, as they could be a precursor to relapse. These thoughts can and should be shared with your partner, sponsor, friend, therapist, or AA acquaintance—any or all of them. Thoughts of drinking that are not shared with another person turn into secrets that are carried, and as these accumulate, a person's risk of drinking increases. You can go on sitting alone with your thoughts of drinking for a little while but time runs out, and when it does—and trust me, it always does—these thoughts will lead you back to drinking. This disease lives in alcoholics and addicts and it welcomes and also encourages these secret thoughts.

My thinking from my lived experience is that on some deep cellular level, once the alcoholic or addict has mentally made the decision to not share their secret thoughts about drinking or their unhealthy behaviour of choice with anyone, the cells deep within him or her, those that are at the centre of the Disease, seem to sense it. The Disease then begins to talk to us. It's almost like it's whispering in our ear. You hear the Disease speaking to you, just as Gazoo did to Fred in the Flintstones. "Yeah ... that's okay ... you don't need to tell anybody. I am here; we can keep this between us." The Disease within tries to trick us back into its clutches. It's almost like an imaginary angel and a devil pop up on our shoulder to try and sway us one way or another when we struggle with doing the right thing. And that is why the disease of alcoholism is described as cunning, baffling and powerful.

So, did I share these types of thoughts before I relapsed? No. I did not share them with anyone, and I did not release them. They became secrets. They accumulated. They built up inside my head. The Disease in me talked to me and told me it was okay. We reunited and I drank. It's almost like making a deal with the devil. And the moment you make one of these little deals, you know it and you can feel it. The conversation you have with yourself around it is viscerally and psychologically uncomfortable.

I remember where I was and what was happening before my last relapse. For the second time, I had close to four months of sobriety under my belt and I had an appointment with my clinical psychologist later that day. For about the previous four weeks I had been having more frequent thoughts of drinking. I couldn't handle the stirrings anymore: I went ahead and made that deal with the devil. The stirrings had built up inside me so much that I knew and accepted my brief stint with sobriety was over. I knew the time to drink was now. I was going to drink that day. I actually bought a coffee from Second Cup just before walking into my session with my therapist. I had no intention of drinking the coffee while I was in my session; I only bought it so that when I left my session, I had one less stop to make before having that first drink and feeling the relief I had been waiting for. I left my session and went straight to the liquor store where I picked up a bottle of wine, as well as two airplane-sized bottles of Grand Marnier and Kahlua. I left the store and once in my car I immediately but discreetly poured the little bottles of what is poison to me into the coffee and took a big sip. Waves of relief rippled through me, but they were mixed with waves of fear and failure. Deep down I knew I was soon going to be in trouble. I isolated myself and drank for about a week and on that final day of drinking, during a blackout, I attempted suicide by taking all of my pills. That would be the last time I had a drink. This last binge-drinking episode and the accompanying suicide attempt scared me even more than ever as I plunged deeper into the darkness and despair of alcoholism.

So, why did I relapse? The answer is, relapse is part of recovery. It only meant I had to work even harder. And, as anyone would, who had just narrowly dodged death once again, I had newfound gratitude around being alive and I felt blessed. I am sure what I did next will come as no surprise; I made the promise to myself and my recovery to not keep any drinking thoughts to myself. I managed to stay sober. By the grace of God, I have not had to go through another relapse. It was the accountability piece that I needed to keep my Disease at bay. This relapse and experience with secret thoughts solidified to me once again the power and importance of truth, as well as the profound meaning of "You are only as sick as your secrets." I adjusted my LiveWell Recipe by giving more importance to specific ingredients, in particular, "Truthful Living" and I just kept at it one day at a time. I had a strong passion to live and survive this deadly disease.

Throughout the rest of my first year of sobriety, I focused on building my LiveWell Recipe and strengthening my newfound relationship with my higher power. I had a lot of healthy fear inside of me during this first year and it was the depth of this raw fear that I would drink again that became the driving force within me. This force helped me stay focused, and to do all that was required of me. It was not just one thing that helped me. It was and still is today the sum total of my whole LiveWell Recipe that helps me stay sober. Each and every ingredient together saved my life.

I often get lost in thought thinking about the vast number of people who have been taken by the disease of addiction. My heart goes out to the still-suffering alcoholic or addict and I am touched especially deeply in this regard when I hear a song by Whitney Houston on the radio. She was an extraordinary American pop singer whose battles with addiction ended with her death in 2012. When I hear her voice I feel close to her soul because we have both been through the excruciating pain and suffering that goes along with addictions. I believe I know what she was feeling.

These moments of realization scare me and shake me because it is a blatant reminder that the disease of alcoholism or a drug addiction never leaves us. It pains me and it scares me when I think of the tragic losses of so many gifted people—like Janis Joplin, Curt Cobain and Amy Winehouse—who died tragically of alcohol and other addictions. There are so many more reminders that this disease lives in a person forever and you just have to keep working hard to keep it under wraps, or you might die. This may sound dramatic, but it is not, as for me to drink is to die. I, and other alcoholics or addicts, must remember that all we get is a daily reprieve. And this cold, hard, truth is why living my LiveWell Recipe is continually saving my life every day.

The Questions to Ask Yourself:
Do I deserve to live a better life?
What is one small thing I can do today that will help me start moving in that direction?

8

Hospitals –WTF?!

I sat leaning forward in the massage chair trying to relax enough to allow the massage therapist to do her job. My arms dangled at my side and the back pain that had brought me to this point in my day was not subsiding. A strange and strong wave of fear and discomfort rushed over me. I felt so light-headed that I was not sure if I could even continue to hold my torso upright, and I almost passed out. The massage therapist stopped working on me and helped me walk over to a bed where I lay down while she went to make me some tea. I lay there for a long time, unable to move. I didn't lose consciousness but I most certainly was on the brink. I felt dizzy, lethargic, and oozy, as though I were about to drift off to sleep.

I had been feeling short of breath and I hadn't felt well overall for a few weeks. Then I began having a hard time getting comfortable while sleeping, and my back felt heavy and achy. It scared me. A lot. I had also been experiencing some chest pain, and when I finally went to the hospital to get checked out, a chest X-ray revealed slight irregular soft, dense tissue in the area of my pulmonary arteries and mild inflammation of the sac surrounding the heart. But it was nothing conclusive. I consulted a friend of mine who was a cardiologist and he suggested I had a case of post-viral pericarditis—the most likely diagnosis for a young and otherwise healthy woman with no cardiac history. My friend suggested I take a course of Naproxen—an anti-inflammatory—and get some rest. I took the Naproxen but passed on the rest.

A week later I was back in the ER with a repeat of the previous week's symptoms. Again I was sent home, but the doctor ordered a couple of heart-related follow-up tests for me. The next day, while working a 12-hour shift in the Intensive Care Unit (ICU) I ran down on my lunch break to undergo a cardiac stress test—which revealed some irregular heartbeats—and an echocardiogram, which revealed some heart valve regurgitation. Regurgitation in the heart is usually caused by leaky valves and shows up as a backflow of blood in a chamber of the heart. Even though both of these findings are highly uncommon in a healthy heart, the regurgitation was slight and the irregular beats could have been caused by stress. As a result, nothing was made of them and no red flags were raised. I went back to the ICU and finished my shift.

The massage appointment represented my effort to ease the back pain that simply would not go away. Once I lay down, it took me a while to get grounded again, and it felt like I needed more air than the atmosphere was providing.

Showing up with No Appointment

Despite the fact that I still did not feel well, I drove myself to my General Practitioner's (GP) office, showing up with no appointment. In hindsight, I probably should not have been driving my car, but when I got to my GP's office, I shared with my doctor my symptoms of chest and back pain, shortness of breath, and an overall feeling of unwellness. He looked at me, assessed me, listened to my heart with his stethoscope, and heard a heart murmur. He sensed there was something seriously wrong with me and decided to send me to the ER for further assessment. I felt a sense of relief when he suggested this to me. It definitely felt like the right thing to do, as something was obviously going on with my health. I went straight home and packed a bag with some essential items before I went to the ER: cell phone charger, laptop, makeup, and more, went into my bag. I didn't know what was in store for me, but deep down I knew I would not be coming home that day. This represented the unassuming, if uncomfortable, beginning of a strange and awful dance with cancer.

You know that feeling where you think you are all free and clear—that there's smooth sailing ahead—and then out of nowhere your life falls apart in staggering fashion and you're standing there wondering what on Earth happened to you? When that happened to me after almost two years of sobriety I felt like my life had stopped completely—dead in its tracks—before taking a hard left in a wild direction at breakneck speed. For the first time in my life, I had been feeling happy, healthy, safe, and secure. In all senses of the word, I was living in holistic wellness. I was working hard to adhere to my LiveWell Recipe for staying physically, mentally, emotionally and spiritually well. When alcoholism nearly takes your life and you are blessed with a second chance, you become overwhelmed with gratitude. The opportunity to live sober, and enjoy that second chance, is not something everybody gets, and I did not take it for granted. I have come to believe that if you are an alcoholic who has found their way to AA, you have been given a special chance. I believe some kind of divine intervention has landed you there. Very few alcoholics enter AA, which makes the process of recovery with this organization similar to winning an immigration lottery. Those who win the lottery are given landed immigrant status and end up with the chance for a new, better life in another country. They are given a little assistance but, for the most part, they have to make a new life all on their own. In the same manner, the alcoholics who make it into the rooms of AA have to do the work necessary to build a new life. And it is no easy ride, for either the immigrant or the alcoholic.

So here I was, I had won the AA lottery. I did the work, I built a new life and now I was ready to live it. At this point, a part of me even I felt like I deserved it. In August of 2013, I was 46 years old and I was about to be diagnosed with cancer. God, Source or Universe had evidently decided I had more work to do.

In fact, I was about to spend the next two months as an inpatient at three different hospitals. I was admitted first to the Cardiac Care Unit at Trillium Health Partners hospital so they could look into "cardiac arrhythmias of unknown cause."

The ER physician was puzzled by my recent ER visit with a diagnosis of pericarditis. By the grace of God, despite the fact there was no strong evidence of a serious problem, the doctor had a hunch something was amiss and he admitted me right then and there.

Paying Attention to the Intuitive Nudges

At the time I didn't place too much significance on the intuitive nudges we all sometimes get, those little voices inside us that point us in the direction we need to go. I had "known" on some level there was something seriously wrong with me, and it had been a knowing that had come to me in the absence of any factual information or "proof." Similarly, there was no evidence in front of the doctor examining me in the ER that I had a problem serious enough to merit admitting me to the hospital. He simply had a "feeling" something was very wrong with me. How lucky I was he followed his intuition in this case! And I wonder now, what kind of world would we live in if everybody had the courage to do the same?

The safety and comfort of being in the hospital gave me some relief and the morphine that was prescribed for me lessened my physical pain. I had not given medical staff a complete and honest health history, as I had left out the part about my alcoholism, and I did so 100% on purpose. As a nurse, I had learned that if I had divulged during my intake triage assessment that I was an alcoholic, the acronym for ethanol—ETOH—would be noted on the front of my chart under "Health History." Those four capital letters would possibly skew the medical staff's perception of who I was, and it would dictate how some of them would treat me. Once you've been labelled an "ETOH" patient, the game changes. Those letters practically glare out at everyone who reads your chart, drawing their attention like a red cape at a bullfight. And, as you can imagine, this information, although technically considered "confidential," soon becomes common knowledge to staff. Since this was one of the hospitals at which I often worked, I wasn't keen on my coworkers finding out this little tidbit of information about me. I was not yet ready for the stigma and judgment I was sure would have been heaped upon me if I had honestly disclosed my alcoholic history.

What's more, I knew the bias health professionals have towards alcoholic patients meant that I would have had to kiss goodbye to the possibility of liberal pain medication. And I was not about to leave my pain management to the mercy of the nurses who had been armed with this fact. I worried they would be more likely to give me lower doses of meds than necessary—along with liberal helpings of judgment and skepticism—each time I requested pain medicine. Of course as health care professionals, we all try to not have bias or judgment interfere with our care and decision making, but the truth is that it is difficult. We are human and the human mind questions.

It's not that I was any saint myself—I know how I used to judge and question the validity of requests for pain medication from an addict or an ETOH patient in my care, and I have witnessed colleagues doing the same thing. I have also overheard colleagues in the ICU discussing patients who were alcoholic. They say things like, "He did this to himself." Or, "She just wants another high." Many medical professionals are surprisingly ignorant about what this disease is really all about and that's why I'm so passionate about sharing my own experience as an alcoholic. Despite the strength I have today in my sobriety, and the integrity of my character, I still at times feel shame about my past and about the fact that I am an alcoholic. This is something that I continue to work on. Self-acceptance. It is a life-long job and it encourages me to step up more. I can't change the past, but I can continually evolve more and more into the person I want to be.

Today, as I continue to heal and grow, keeping my past as an alcoholic secret is becoming less important to me. The writing of this book and the launch of my signature yoga therapy program (called "Tina's Recovery Yoga," or *TRY*) is putting the truth about my alcoholism increasingly on public display. People's views about addicts are gradually changing, but it's slow work. People are starting to understand addiction as more of a disease, like diabetes or heart disease, rather than as a personal weakness. I see people treat alcoholics and addicts with greater compassion. But there is still judgment, disdain, stigma, and shame directed towards alcoholics and people still assume addictive behaviour is a decision. It's my hope this book will help educate people and shift our communities towards better understanding and awareness around addictions. Speaking from experience, the truth is I no more chose to be an alcoholic than I chose to have cancer. It is my hope and wish, one that comes from deep in my soul, that in my lifetime I may see continued shifts and improved awareness and understanding about the Disease of addiction.

Asleep in a Blurry Haze of Fear and Morphine

During that first night of hospitalization, I slept in a blurry haze of fear and morphine. The following morning a new panel of blood work was ordered, as well as more investigative tests. The first diagnostic test done the following morning was another echocardiogram to examine my heart, with particular emphasis paid to the strength and efficiency of each beat. The test showed slight irregularities, but it was inconclusive again. Inconclusive was beginning to feel like a broken record. Next, I was taken down to the radiology department for a CT scan of my chest and thorax.

This is the point of my story I don't think I will ever get used to sharing without flashes of terror. I do not remember going down to radiology that day, I do not remember returning to my hospital room, and I do not remember being told I had a large mass in my chest. The CT scan found a large anterior and mid-mediastinal mass that was 7.3 cm in diameter and creating notable compression of my left main pulmonary artery.

WHOA … in layman's terms, it meant there was a whopper of a tumour on the front of my heart that was so large that it was pressing on both of my pulmonary arteries (the blood vessels that feed blood to the lungs) enough to impede blood flow. At 7.3 centimetres in diameter, which is almost three inches, the tumour was about as wide as a crayon is long or, put another way, it was exactly the diameter of a regulation hardball.

I believe there is an "Anatomy of the Spirit" that is driven by the energy contained in everything we experience, see and feel in our day-to-day lives. While some of our experiences are happy and they carry positive energy, some are painful and they carry negative energy. This can sometimes affect our physical and mental bodies adversely. Negative emotions and the negative energy they impart can have a cumulative effect on the body, and over time manifest as a physical ailment. That is where clichés like "it will catch up with you" come from. We can only handle so much and at some point, the level of negative energy in our bodies reaches a tipping point. It ultimately wears down the normal, healthy functioning of our cells.

I had an academically-oriented medical understanding and wasn't focused on the energetic aspects of disease at the time. But I now believe the cancer in me started at a point when I was vulnerable. I had endured an enormous amount of emotional pain and I simply couldn't handle any more. The majority of my pain was centred in and around my heart, making it a vulnerable area. I believe cancer cells are opportunistic and all it took was one circulating cancer cell to sense this vulnerability and attach there. Once attached, there was no looking back; there was a cancer journey ahead. Six years after all this unfolded it is still sometimes difficult to think, write, and talk about it all. It still seems a little crazy and I am somewhat bewildered at times. Sometimes I think, "Did that really happen?!" And sometimes, when I pause and think about my cancer journey, I experience vivid sensory flashbacks of how painful it all was. When I allow my mind to take me back to that time and place,

I feel a heavy energetic field radiating around and out from my heart. It is such a weighty excruciating feeling. I can feel both the pain I went through during the worst days of cancer and also the pain I experienced as a young child, which had led to the manifestation of the tumour in the first place. Again, I think; the body does keep score.

The Body Keeps Score

I was steered to that idea by a book I came across titled *The Body Keeps the Score: Brain, Mind, and Body in the Healing of Trauma*. Written by Bessel Van Der Kolk, M.D., the book validates the impact trauma has on the body and identifies the need for recovery. It talks about how neglect can wire children to be on high alert, and continuously tune their stressed bodies to a "fight or flight" response. I totally relate to that statement, as it describes my entire childhood. Another statement in the book I totally relate to as an adult addresses how some individuals may strive to achieve a "numbed out" state to keep demons at bay and protect themselves from future trauma. These observations describe how my body felt, and confirm that the strategies I later employed to try to cope and manage in my day-to-day life were "normal," under the circumstances. The million-dollar question was: Was it too late for me? That's what I was thinking. All those years of hard drinking in a toxic world. Was the score my body had been keeping for all those years too high for me to even? Was I up against too much? Should I give up? As I have already shared, my unhealthy coping strategies had almost killed me. It was not until I got sober, learned proper coping skills, and started to work through some of my pain that I was able to start to thrive. But now, here I was at a new juncture and it was becoming clear to me now that I had been on a bumpy journey of self-discovery, both during my descent into alcoholism and during the difficult climb to sobriety thereafter.

When I first learned of the CT scan results, and could consciously process them, I was mostly in a state of disbelief. There was a tumour in my body—and on my heart, of all places! I'd heard many stories of people surviving different types of cancer in different areas of the body, but the heart … do such cases even exist? To this day, I know very little about the kind of tumour I had. I don't want to potentially dampen the quality of the life remaining to me by reviewing the details of my illness and embedding them into my brainstem. I am alive, and I have faith. The larger and more interesting question that cannot be denied here, is "Why there?" And is it possible there is something symbolic about where the cancer chose to take up residence in my body? Some people may say this mass was put in place to shield me from pain, as a form of protection to soften the intensity of the emotional pain I had been up against as a child. It hurts me today to think of the troubles that Tina as a young child, a young girl, and a teenager endured. I do believe the mass manifested itself in my body due to pain. When I look back at myself as a four-year-old child, I can see how fearful I was, how frightened and confused. But even at that very young age, I learned to put on a brave face and act like everything was okay.

Acting Like Everything Was Okay

So, fast forward a few decades to see me lying in a hospital bed with a large cancerous mass in my chest, and I was still acting like everything was okay. I do not remember much of that first week as I must have gone into a state of shock. I didn't want to feel anything or face what was going on, and I was a little resistant to processing what was happening to me. I was also medicated with high doses of morphine, and this put me into a numbed state of existence. What I was going through right then was the sort of thing you would hope to only see happening to someone in a movie, but right now, it was actually happening to me. We never really think these kinds of things can happen to us, but they can, and they do. It did. With the diagnosis in place, a multiplicity of tests was completed in a flurry. I underwent numerous blood tests, a needle biopsy of the mass, and a bone marrow test.

I had quickly reverted back to my old and engrained coping mechanisms and all I wanted in those moments was to not feel. None of the Cardiac Care Unit (CCU) nurses who were looking after me knew I was an alcoholic and they were dumbfounded by the amount of morphine my little body could handle. My history as an alcoholic means I can tolerate a ridiculously high amount of drugs and alcohol. Once upon a time, I had checked myself into a hospital for treatment of my fourth alcohol withdrawal episode and I had been surprised when doctors placed me on a Mental Health hold, which is called a "Form 1." This allowed staff to hold me against my will for up to 72 hours while I was assessed to see if I was at risk to harm myself or others. I had been binge drinking for days and I was so sick I couldn't even drink anymore. I went to the hospital because the alcohol was leaving my system, and I became terribly afraid that I would have an alcohol withdrawal seizure, as I had had before. I had known I was at risk and I needed medical intervention so I had called a taxi to take me to the ER. I had immediately told the triage nurse I was in alcohol withdrawal and that my heart was racing. The usual battery of tests and interventions were done for a typical ETOH withdrawal. An intravenous feed was started to give me fluids, and blood was drawn to check my electrolytes, liver function and my alcohol level. As a result of years of alcoholic drinking, my tolerance for The Drink had risen so high that I could drink as much as a horse. My alcohol level came back in the lethal, toxic range. In acute alcohol intoxication, the blood ethanol level is typically elevated to 100 to 300 mg/dL

Normal findings: 0-50 mg/dL

Critical Values: > 300 mg/dL

The alcohol level of my blood was greater than 300 that day. Despite the fact that I was still standing. the attending physician put me on a Mental Health hold.

Chronic alcoholics can commonly have blood alcohol

levels higher than 300 mg/dL and they can begin to show signs of alcohol withdrawal even at elevated levels.[18] That evening, I was walking and talking with a blood alcohol level well over 300; this could only mean I was abusing alcohol and I was endangering myself.

The physician working the ER that night understood what my blood alcohol level meant; I was at risk of having alcohol withdrawal seizures, liver damage, brain damage or, even worse, a cold, sad, miserable death. The physician did the right thing, and he meant well by putting me on a Form 1 that day, but I was not helped at all. This is the point in an alcoholic's trajectory where I would like to see our health care system intervene and offer some real, concrete help: medically managed withdrawal and immediate transfer to a rehab program. Instead, my purse and all of my belongings were taken away from me and I was left alone in a room. I had already been treated for withdrawal but was now waiting for a psych doctor to determine if I could be legally or safely discharged.

Convincing the Psychiatrist I Was in No Danger

If I wanted to get out of the ER and go home I had to convince the psychiatrist I was not a danger to myself. My blood alcohol level clearly showed I was. The psychiatrist arrived to assess me and determine if I was safe to be discharged. I told him that I was aware of my situation, and aware I had a drinking problem, and I rattled off fictitious details about all the support I had around me. I basically told him what I knew he needed to hear. At this point, it had been around eight hours since my last drink, and although I was being treated with benzodiazepine, I was dying for a drink. I lied to get out of there and after I was discharged, I clambered into a taxi and had the driver stop at a liquor store before taking me home.

---

[18] EBM Consult.com, https://www.ebmconsult.com/articles/lab-test-ethanol-alcohol-level?action=search&search_box=alcohol%20levels%20in%20the%20blood&search_within=&type_of_searc accessed November 4, 2019

The body and the mind have indescribably powerful cravings to drink while withdrawing from alcohol. What makes the situation more complex are the feelings of guilt, shame, and remorse the alcoholic feels over what they had done the night before. The fact I had had a binge bad enough to land myself in the hospital on a Form 1 filled me with an unspeakable amount of anguish and despair. The need for me to drink was off the charts. I can still remember that taxi ride home from the hospital that day. I don't even want to know what I looked like to the taxi driver, but in that moment, I didn't care. Actually, that is not accurate. The truth was, I couldn't care. The physical withdrawal and my diseased mind had, again, defeated me.

God, how I wish I had had immediate options for treatment in the many moments of despair I experienced during my drinking years. It is in those moments of desperation that the alcoholic is receptive and deep in his or her soul they truly want help. These are the rare windows where we actually might say, "I give up," and, "help me." I wish when the psychiatrist came in to assess me I had been immediately offered a bed in a treatment centre. I was desperate for help and vulnerable; this was a lost opportunity to actually treat my Disease.

Many alcoholics have had similar experiences. They take themselves off to a treatment program in the city where they are living while in that raw, desperate, vulnerable state, and they ask for help. These people are inevitably told to come back a week to two weeks later so they can be properly processed and admitted. One week to a person in such a desperate state could be life threatening. It is my hope that immediate treatment options will be made available in the future as part of the normal treatment protocol for alcoholics in withdrawal.

I am grateful that, at the time of my cancer diagnosis, I was sober, and committed to living a life of sobriety. It honestly scares me to think of how all of this might have played out had I not been sober. All I can say is everything happened in Divine timing. After the initial shock-and-fear phase of my cancer diagnosis wore off, I began to emerge from my morphine-clouded state and the situation became real. What? Cancer? Seriously? Me? Cancer? Is this for real? I remember looking back over my life as if it were a movie, viewing it scene by scene, as if in slow motion. At the same time, it was almost as if the movie of my life were stuck in "fast forward" mode as my brain rapidly scanned through the years of my life. I remembered all the circumstances I had endured and overcome. The situations I had survived, the adversity I had pushed through. I had been led by what I call my "inner spirit drive" to keep trudging ahead and do the next right thing to make things better for me. I had made it through life thus far. For God's sake, I had survived the Disease of alcoholism. All that, and now it's over, just like that? The friends who knew how hard I had worked to overcome my past, get sober and remain sober, reacted with shock. It seemed so wrong and unfair. But the cancer was real, and in the long run, it wasn't unfair or wrong at all, it was fair, and it was all right. In fact, it was a surprisingly graceful, transformative experience.

The first week of my cancer journey was a nightmare. Not only did I have a mass in my chest, but the physicians on my case had difficulty diagnosing me. At first, I was told I had deadly T-Cell Lymphoma ... which is grim and not a diagnosis anyone would want. I interpreted this as meaning I was truly going to die. The next day the physicians/pathologist changed the diagnosis ... I can't even remember what the second diagnosis was, but it was not a lethal one. I remember my clinical psychologist saying, "we can work with this, we can work with this one." The short version of my two-week stay at Trillium was that I was misdiagnosed twice and I was no closer to knowing what kind of tumour I had. What I did know was the tumour was large, leukemic in nature and nobody knew if I was going to live or die. Because of the inconclusive nature of the medical staff's assessments and their difficulty in diagnosing my condition, I secured a "rush" appointment with Princess Margaret Hospital's (PMH) Leukemia Rapid Assessment Clinic. I was now two weeks into this nightmare and I still had no idea what was going on. I was beginning to freak out. I felt grateful to have friends who were willing to take charge and arrange for me to have a bed in Mount Sinai's Cardiac Care Unit (CCU). Knowing this was in the works, I kindly asked for my chart from the nurse who was assigned to me at Trillium and I went off in search of answers and treatment at PMH and Mount Sinai. I didn't tell my nurse I would not be returning to my room at Trillium Health Partners after my appointment at PMH. There is a lot of administration involved in discharging someone from the hospital and I was worried my discharge would make me late for my urgent PMH appointment. My friend Kristina and I "Thelma-and-Louised-it" out of there. I sat in a wheelchair with my chart in hand and Kristina ran as fast as she could through the hospital parking lot pushing me ahead of her. It was such a liberating moment. We laughed and laughed.

The Question to Ask Yourself:
Do I look at all challenges as opportunities to grow? Or do I think, "Why Me?"

9

Fear and Uncertainty at Mount Sinai Hospital

Despite the laughter, I remember how full of fear and anger I was when I arrived at Princess Margaret Hospital for a 10:00 a.m. appointment with an oncology specialist at the Leukemia Rapid Assessment Clinic named Dr. Schuh. I was feeling weary and very frightened about what lay ahead for me.

Dr. Schuh, who would later become the oncologist in charge of my case, came into my life after two weeks of testing, waiting, plenty of physical and mental pain, two wrong diagnoses, and, let's not forget, the knowledge I had a large mass in my chest. I was in a state of limbo and looking death in the face. The tumour was limiting blood flow to my lungs so I became short of breath very easily; my friend Kristina wheeled me up to the registration desk in my wheelchair to sign in and complete the necessary paperwork prior to getting my blood work done. I was now in Cancer Land, and this realization hit me hard. I really *did* have cancer and I was now in a hospital full of people who were just like me! I sat there and looked around at all the people with little beanie cancer hats on. There were bald, sickly, frail-looking people all around me. And I thought … OH NO … NO, NO, NO! I am NOT joining this club, too! I felt anger bubbling up and I felt like I was losing control. I had a conversation with God and this is what I said:

"Look, God, I'm good with the AA thing and I am resigned to my lifelong membership there. I accept that I am an alcoholic and I am okay with that. I am a lifetime member of that club, but come on, I don't want *this* club too."

I was angry, I was scared, and I didn't like what was going on around me. I didn't like what was happening to my body. I was steadily losing control and no longer in denial. I was feeling like my life was slipping away from me. Self-Pity—Anger's cousin—had kicked into high gear. I was thinking things like, "Why me? Why now?" And the answer was, "Why *Not Me*?!"

I looked around at the collection of ill people surrounding me, feeling exhausted and discouraged, and I said to my friend "I don't know if I want to let anybody do any more tests on me today." I understood enough of what was going on to know that I had become a difficult case to diagnose and there would be more tests; they would probably need another bone marrow specimen. I was terrified of another bone marrow procedure. The doctor who had performed the first one must not have done many, as it was so painful I squealed like a wounded animal. He actually noted in his chart that it had been a traumatic procedure, and it took a long time for the site to heal.

I sat in the small assessment room at PMH and watched Dr. Schuh read the physician's notes and the test results on my chart from Trillium. The seconds hung in the air like minutes as I waited for him to say something. Deep down I was hoping he would magically say there had been a mistake and I didn't have cancer after all, but of course, that didn't happen. He finally rattled off the summary of my case: two incorrect diagnoses, a lack of complete testing on previous samples, the inconclusiveness of it all ... and then he paused. He looked at me and said, "This is F$%&#D up." Well, I have to say I connected with him in that very moment. He was now speaking my language, the language of complete truth. Dr. Schuh then went on to say we had to start all over with the testing. The testing done at Trillium lacked some necessary information and what was there was of no value, so we got right to it. The first order of business was another bone marrow procedure, and because I already trusted Dr. Schuh, I let him do it. It was a completely different experience from the first barbaric experience I had endured. I was grateful to discover that he was highly skilled and competent. A complete battery of tests was ordered and done, as well as a second biopsy. I was then transferred from Princess Margaret Hospital to the

Mount Sinai Cardiac Care Unit and settled into my new room to wait for my test results and my diagnosis. During this time, I maintained my composure and to be honest, I was somewhat hopeful a miracle would happen. Either that or I was delusional, I am not sure. What I do remember of this transition from one hospital to the other was that I was scared and I didn't feel like I fit in anywhere. I felt a bit like the recorder on my life was operating in slow motion. Physically I moved more slowly than usual because I was at risk of a cardiac injury, but it was much more than that. It was like I was walking around in No Man's Land. It was surreal and I felt alone. The rest of the world was going on about their business as usual but it was not business as usual for me. I was gridlocked in time and space and waiting for a diagnosis. I was, in some fundamental ways, waiting to meet my maker. I felt alone, lost and afraid. It was a really strange place to be.

My Heart was in a Tough Spot

Being in the medical profession, I understood my heart was in a tough spot. It had to share its sacred space with a mass the width of a baseball. A mass that I am sure was not warm and fuzzy. I imagined it to be dark, gloomy, cold, unfriendly and frightful. Despite the reality of my grave situation, I tried to stay positive but I think most people around me thought my days were numbered. I mean, who survives having a large tumour invading their heart? That conversation was the elephant in the room. Nobody wanted to say anything to me out loud, and I didn't know what to make of any of it. So I downplayed the magnitude of the situation and put that brave face of mine on again.

What I did know was I had to keep doing things to help keep my head and spirits up. I followed my LiveWell Recipe as much as I could, and what a blessing it was to have already been living a life of recovery. I ramped up my daily deposits into wellness and took the steps necessary in order to offset the unimaginable mental stress I was now under. I don't even really remember how stressful it all was. I just dug in and did the things I needed to do to make it through each day. And make it through each day I did. I have to say that with the help of my LiveWell Recipe I managed pretty well, but it was due to much more than the magic work of the Recipe. Yes, I was pretty scared inside, and I wore a brave face, but it was different from the brave face I put on for the world around me when I had been a little girl. The faith I now had and was experiencing allowed me to access courage from within and I was actually feeling brave, just like the lion at the end of the movie, *The Wizard of Oz*.

As time had passed, and I continued to make efforts to connect spiritually, something had started to change. It was as if I actually *became* okay, and I wasn't just pretending. This is the part I cannot explain. I started to shift into a zone that was no longer based on fear; it was based on hope, faith, and positivity. In this difficult time, I turned to my LiveWell Recipe like it was a life-saving medicine. My thoughts were all about what I could do in the moment to help me get through this more easily. What could I do *now* to feel better? I prayed, meditated and just kept putting one foot in front of the other. And, yes, I was still scared—I mean, who wouldn't be? There is a trembling fear a cancer patient feels that is so hard to rightfully describe. It engulfs you and you feel it, yet you are numb. You have no choice but to be with it and you carry on. So many others like me sit in this limbo, waiting, in the fear and the wonder of each and every cancer diagnosis.

What I ultimately did manage to do was to stop dwelling in fear and start thinking of the future. It is quite amazing to look back at this period in my life and think about it. I never specifically asked to come out of the "fear fog" I was in. I believe it happened organically, partly as a result of my efforts to feel better on my own, and partly because of God's own grace. I settled into a spiritually-based state, and although prayer was a part of my LiveWell Recipe and had been designed to keep me sober, it now took on an added layer of meaning. The weekend before my hospital admission I had been at a summer learning camp in the beautiful Finger Lakes region of New York State. I had been studying the philosophy of yoga with one of my favorite teachers, Dr. Douglas Brooks. I love studying with this brilliant man because his teaching of Rajanaka Yoga[19] invites his students to investigate themselves more deeply, and in doing so gain insight into how we might achieve a deeper engagement with life itself. While at this training I learned a special and powerful Kali Mantra Prayer. Kali is a fierce feminine goddess and the destroyer of evil. With ferocity—like Kali herself, in fact—I recited this prayer as I stepped into my own battle with "evil" once again. The prayer goes like this:

OM HRIM KSAM

BHAKSA JVALA JIHVE

KARALA DAMSTRE

PRATYANGIRE

KSAM HRIM HUM PHAT

To this day, I still recite the Kali prayer on a daily basis, and I probably always will. It came to me in a time of need, and I embraced it and placed sacred meaning on it. Now I have no wish to let its magic powers go.

During my week as an inpatient at Mount Sinai Hospital, I was granted some two-hour passes to leave the hospital. In the headspace that I was in—marked by feeling both fear and deep abiding faith—all I really wanted to do was attend an AA meeting. They are part of my LiveWell Recipe and during this stressful time of crisis, I actually had a yearning to attend. The feeling of connection and the spiritual energy at meetings helped me immensely during this time. If you have ever been to an AA meeting, you will know there is an indescribable

---

[19] Rajanaka, A Tradition of Auspicious Wisdom, http://rajanaka.com/, accessed November 24, 2019

spiritual energy present that you cannot help but tap into. I felt supported, comforted, loved, and connected, not only to the members of my AA group, but also to something bigger than myself. In fact, these meetings were a crucial part of helping me remain in a spiritual state and, for the most part, those feelings of overwhelming fear never came back. My friend, Kerri, and her partner, Brock, would pick me up, take me to my meetings and then bring me back to the hospital. They were amazing.

Estranged from My Family and Friends

While waiting for a definitive diagnosis I was surprised by an unexpected visitor: a former friend with whom I had broken ties while I had been removing toxic people, places, and things from my life during the early stages of my sobriety. She had learned of my illness through a yoga studio we had both attended and she showed up at the hospital one day. She had not been invited, and she showed up unannounced; her company was unwanted. With as much composure and calmness as I could muster, I looked this person—who I had not seen for nearly two years—straight in the eye. And I said to her, "I may or may not be dying, I don't know, but my death bed wish is that you DO NOT contact my family." Despite my wishes, this person selfishly took it upon herself to contact my family and ultimately there was more anxiety heading my way after she did.

Although I know she meant me no harm, it was still like a scene out of a bad movie. When people who lack the capacity for empathy attempt to be helpful, they often end up imposing themselves on you and barging into your experience. People who are fighting an illness are vulnerable and don't typically have the energy or emotional resources to fight for their rights. When someone injects themselves into someone else's personal battle, with a total disregard for their actual needs, it can be especially trying.

This wasn't the only person I had invited out of my life. I

had also chosen to become estranged from my father, my two brothers, and two girlfriends from my childhood. I had not reached out to any of them when I had become sick, nor did I have any intention of involving them in my life. It created a moral and emotional dilemma for me. Even though I was estranged from these people there was a part of me that wished they were there for me. In the deeply vulnerable state that I was in, I did want my family. Who wouldn't? And deciding to lock them out of my life was tough. But what I wanted was a version of my family that didn't exist, and I knew I had to stay conscious of the fact that what they offered me was not what I needed for my healing. In the interest of supporting my healing sober journey, and making decisions that were in the best interest of Tina long term, I resisted inviting my family into my cancer experience. I chose to not re-engage.

In the meantime, I waited for my test results. After a week of waiting, the physicians at Mount Sinai and Princess Margaret Hospital had come to an agreement about my diagnosis. Both Dr. Schuh from PMH and Dr. Christensen from the ICU at Mount Sinai came to my room together to give me the news. I remember the moment that they both walked into my room. They came in together, as a team, with serious looks on their faces, both of which clued me into the fact that the news wasn't good. The diagnosis was Myeloid Sarcoma, leukemic in nature. I can still see this conversation vividly. There I am, sitting on my bed with my knees hugged to my chest, and there are the two doctors, sitting against the wall at the foot of the bed. I had just been told conclusively that I had a cancerous tumour and it now had a name, Myeloid Sarcoma. I initially remained calm throughout the discussions and it may have been some of the strangest few moments I have ever experienced. The two physicians struggled a little as they delivered the news, almost as if they were in a play and at times it felt as if they had forgotten their lines.

I wasn't retaining all of what was being said to me, but the tipping point for me which I clearly remembered was when I asked them one pointed question: "Will I lose my hair?" Dr. Schuh said, "Yes," at which point I dropped my head and sobbed. I loved my hair, but it really wasn't even about the hair, I was just scared of the uncertain path ahead of me. Being told that I would lose my hair made the cancer diagnosis real. This blob in my chest was not just going to fade away on its own, as I had been wishing in moments of delusion. I agreed to the chemotherapy treatment that was suggested right then and there and the paperwork was completed immediately. These guys weren't messing around. They also asked me if I wanted them to post a "DNR" order on my chart. DNR means "Do Not Resuscitate" in the event of heart, lung, or brain failure. As a nurse, I realized that the precarious location of the tumour meant that chemotherapy could set in motion fatal complications. I signed the DNR, although the fact that I was only 46 years old made me hesitate. People my age should not be signing or agreeing to this, but I knew it was the right decision for my situation.

That night in bed I cried as I drew myself into the tiniest ball I could manage and hid under my blankets. I used to do the same thing as a child when the pain got to be too much. I was trying to comfort myself as best I could, and I was also trying to hide from the disruptions going on around me, if only for a private moment or two. The intense emotional pain I was feeling that night in the hospital was not new for me, as I felt like a child again, frightened and alone. A little while later the nurse came in and I was grateful for the dose of morphine she gave me so I could drift off to sleep.

An Interesting Medical Case

The next day my room filled with residents eager to learn about my case. A resident is a doctor who has graduated from medical school but is completing additional training for a specialization in a particular area of medicine under the supervision of a senior doctor. The fact that I was a healthy

46-year-old woman with a tumour the width of a baseball sitting on her heart made me an interesting medical case, especially for residents. While this team of young doctors discussed my case at my bedside, they mentioned the literature they had read about Myeloid Sarcoma. I immediately, and with a sense of urgency, asked them if I could have a copy of what they had read. There was a heavy pause. They all looked at each other as if to say ... "Should we?" They clearly felt this might not be a good idea and only hesitantly concluded that it would be okay. An hour later, the promised packet of papers I had requested was delivered to me.

I stared at the heavy packet as my mind processed what I actually held in my hand. I remember the crazy amount of emotion rushing through me as I started reading the first couple of paragraphs. And then I stopped. A voice inside me said, "What are you doing?" I asked myself what knowing more about Myeloid Sarcoma would do for me. Or, more specifically, how it would affect my mind. I also asked myself if I needed to know what my odds of living or dying were, based on reading about other people's experiences. What was in it for me? Ultimately I chose not to go down that path. I put the packet down, never to attempt to read it again. I also chose to never Google anything about my tumour or about Myeloid Sarcoma. To this day I still know very little about it, except for one thing, and that is, it will not take my life.

As it turned out, the type of tumour I had was known to erode surrounding tissues. Great. Why on God's Green Earth the doctors had chosen to share this of all details with me, I do not know. But, there I was, with a large tumour situated on the front of my heart and it was pressing on both of my pulmonary arteries. I fervently hoped it was not already busily eating away at the surrounding tissue. It meant that there was a chance that I could bleed out—another way of saying "to die rapidly"— almost immediately once chemotherapy began to take effect.

So now the doctors faced the dilemma of deciding which hospital was qualified to take responsibility for my care, all based on the fact that I might bleed to death when the chemotherapy started. PMH was declining to take me as they were not equipped for or experienced in critical care. The CCU at Mount Sinai could no longer treat me, as they were not qualified to administer chemotherapy. The ICU had agreed to accept me, but since I had worked in that ICU in recent years, staff had to ask me if I was comfortable being actively cared for by previous colleagues. The option to be moved across the street to Toronto General Hospital was given. At this point, I really didn't care who was caring for me so I gave the go-ahead to be transferred up to the ICU at Mount Sinai. Just before I was transferred to the ICU somebody involved in the chain of dialogue about the possibility of me bleeding out pointed out that if this were to happen during my first round of chemotherapy, there was not an ICU in the world that would be able to save me. Period, full stop. The decision was made to send me off to PMH, instead. It was a bit of a whirlwind, but nothing I couldn't handle, as my mind fixated on the lifesaving chemotherapy that awaited me. Anyone who has been struck with a cancer diagnosis can relate to the fact that it is a crash course in uncertainty. I took great comfort in having a conclusive diagnosis and I was eager to move forward with the next phase of my cancer journey, but there was one thing I couldn't shake: the elephant in the room. It came with me from Trillium Hospital to Mt. Sinai and now to Princess Margaret, and its name was "Uncertainty." As we all know, the word just does not have a good rap. It's very seldom used in a positive context, and it doesn't have any positive connotations attached to it. The uncertainty of our life on Earth really is just not something we talk about much, or really even think about. Most of us are oblivious to the precariousness of this precious gift of a life we are living. But the truth is, as human beings, we all live with uncertainty, and we're in a constant state of the unknown. Before my experiences with alcoholism and cancer, I, like many people, took life for granted. I did not realize the uncertainty of it all. But the truth is, there really are no guarantees in this life. And for me, at this juncture, my chances of staying alive were not looking so good. I didn't know if I would make it through this life storm, and nobody dared to talk about the risks I faced. I had to learn to live with this elephant and I began to look at uncertainty on a whole new level.

I had assuredly faced "Uncertainty" when I had danced with the devil of death during my battle with alcoholism. So I did grasp that I was lucky to even be alive. But there is something different about the nature of uncertainty when it comes to cancer. As many of us do eventually, I had to come to terms with the fact that uncertainty is part of living. And I did it by turning to my faith. Faith was the only thing that had power over the elephant of my potentially impending death. Faith carried me and comforted me and helped to deflate the elephant in my room.

The Question to Ask Yourself:

Am I in any fear right now, and if so, am I willing to pray, or meditate, so I can move into the comfort of faith?

10

Hospital #3—Princess Margaret

I packed up my room at Mount Sinai Hospital and was transferred through a connecting hallway to Princess Margaret Hospital (PMH) where I was admitted into the Malignant Hematology Unit. Malignant Hematology Unit .... Really. I actually took a picture of the placard on the wall on a return visit as a sort of "Yes, this really did happen." The name sounded like some sort of doomsday prophecy and, honestly, I think they should consider changing it. It had now been about four weeks since my health issues had begun, and this was my third hospital. The next leg of my cancer journey awaited.

I think of Princess Margaret as a beehive because from Monday to Friday it is buzzing, buzzing, on each and every floor. It is an open concept hospital, which gives great visibility to its internal workings. If you look inward from each floor you can see the hustle and movement on all of the other levels. The flurry of activity is incredible as health care professionals can be seen everywhere saving the lives of so many cancer patients. And then on the weekends, it's the strangest thing; almost all activity stops and the place feels like a factory beset by layoffs. I never felt comfortable going down to get a coffee during the weekend hours at the restaurant on the hospital's main level, possibly because there was just no life in the building during those times and I was there to *save* my life.

When I first got to PMH I sat quietly alone in my new room, in a place nobody would ever want to be or think they will ever find themselves. I was now an inpatient at Princess Margaret Hospital, one of the world's leading cancer centres, and I was about to start a course of chemotherapy. WOW. "How did I get here?" I wondered. Although I had had about a month to process this new threat to my body, I was still experiencing a matrix of strong emotions. I was feeling comforted to have a conclusive diagnosis, and I was also very excited to get on with it. I was grateful my feelings and emotions had shifted and my fears were suppressed by the strong faith that permeated my every cell. It was actually kind of strange that I wasn't worried that I might bleed out when the chemotherapy started. I wasn't catastrophizing about how that might all play out, and I wasn't at all feeling like I was going to die. It still surprises me to this day how calm and full of faith I felt. On some level, I knew I was going to live. Which was odd, since all the odds were clearly against me. Even six years later, and now cured, it's still crazy to even think of having had an oncologist. I mean let's face it, it's never a good thing to say "My oncologist ... " I honestly still can't believe I had one. How could I not have been freaking out? The only rationale behind the calm I felt was that I was connected to something bigger than myself and spiritually carried during this time. As part of my LiveWell recipe, I had been engaged in daily rituals to keep myself spiritually fit and sober. I was grateful now that the result of my efforts to stay spiritually fit was that I was in a kind of spiritual alignment with my situation. I also came to believe this alignment led to channels within me being open, which led to grace flowing in. And I chose to believe miracles do happen.

As often happened, my dear friend, Kelly, appeared in my new hospital room in a very timely manner; literally minutes later it was time to start the IV administration of the chemotherapy drugs. Two drugs had been prescribed for me and they were to be administered together to break down the malignant tumour that had invaded my body. It was just like a classic scene right out of a movie, and it even felt as if things were happening in slow motion. The nurse came into the quiet room, serious and somber, and she started to prepare the drugs for administration. There was not a lot of talking. But while in the midst of giving me instructions, and programming the IV pump, in fact just before she pressed the start button on the IV pump, the nurse looked at both Kelly and me and said, "What matters will change." And change it did.

Do We Really Control Our Lives?

I had already changed and grown so much since beating alcoholism and making it through to almost two years of sobriety. I had learned we really don't control much of what goes on in our lives, we can try and mess with it, but it really is all part of God's plan. I had also come to accept the other part of that concept, which is our life isn't always the way we want it to be, yet it shows up exactly the way we need it to be, and it unfolds exactly as it should. At the time, however, lying in that hospital bed with an IV pump at my side, there was nothing more for me to do than to turn it all over to God and let it all unfold.

Just as if it were part of a script, the nurse pressed "Start" on the IV pump and Drug A started dripping its way into my veins. Next, she connected a very large syringe to the lower port of the IV tubing to inject Drug B "push style" (which means fast). The odd sense of calm I was feeling didn't last for long, as almost immediately I felt as though I were on a rollercoaster with many twists, turns, and free falls. The first few days of chemotherapy were a little traumatic. I lay there during the initial phase of the infusion while the drug and my body were busy saving my life. I was not yet affected by any of the unpredictable and terrible side effects chemotherapy can bring, and I was awake, aware, and feeling pretty good. I was grateful to still have my wits about me at this time, as both my brother and my father—both of them still estranged from me—showed up randomly and separately in my hospital room. Remember me asking my former friend to not inform my family? *Wish Not Granted!* First, my brother showed up, and it was by no means a healthy visit replete with delightful exchanges of love and support.

My roommate, Karen, immediately sensed that this was not your typical brother-sister visit. She felt an energy that made her feel like I might need some help with this situation, and she actually pushed the call bell to bring the nurse. Remember,

I had not asked my brother to visit me and I did not want him there. He said, "You can't go through this without letting at least some of us in." He almost pleaded with me, as though he had a right to be there. I knew in that moment that I had to put myself first, and his presence wasn't making me feel good. I looked at him calmly, and from a deep place of spiritual comfort, and said. "I am not alone. Just go." To say that this was hard for me to do is an enormous understatement.

Yet, as difficult as it was, and as much as part of me desperately wanted him there, deep down I knew that although he would try, he did not know how to be there for me. I naturally wished I had a family that could rally around me but I knew that scenario was just a fantasy. Part of my self-care at this juncture was to focus on healing while keeping my recovery front and centre. For good reason, it was important to me that my family understood my priorities and that they were no longer a part of them. I was not going to indulge their need to be able to say they were there for me when what they had to offer, or how they would be able to show up for me, would cause me pain and could put me at risk. I didn't have the space or energy to look after anyone else at this time, as I was fighting for my life and the maintenance of my sobriety. "Just go," I had said.

It pained me to hurt him in this way and I was so sad to turn my brother away, but I am grateful to this day to have had such strong resolve in such a vulnerable moment. It was the right decision. A decision that was good for Tina.

Working with My Psychologist

I had developed this strength and resolve through my work with the amazing clinical psychologist, Dr. Stephanie Bot. It had been through my work with her that I had found the courage to go through the sharp pains of self-discovery and to access the strength within to make good decisions when faced with a tough situation.

My brother's unexpected and unwanted visit during my time of healing brought painful emotions up from deep within the vault of my heart, unleashing negative, toxic energy into my space. After he left I was terrified this bad energy would stay with me on a physical level and my thoughts went kind of crazy, as they were driven by both my beliefs and my fears. I thought I had been working to free myself of bad old energy and sickness by treating my cancer, only to be hit with this new blast of what I perceived to be harmful energy from my brother. I believed that a build-up of painful, negative emotions from my heart had caused my cancer. So I prayed. I prayed fervently, and I repeated this Mantra:

"Dear God, please do not let any negative energy deposit itself in my physical body."

"Dear God, please do not let any negative energy deposit itself in my physical body."

"Dear God, please do not let any negative energy deposit itself in my physical body."

In my heart of hearts, and deep down in my soul, I knew the mass that lived inside my body and on my heart had been caused by painful negative emotions and it was, at that very moment, disintegrating. Each minute that passed meant more of it was leaving me and, by God, I was not going to let it come back again!

My next surprise visitor was my father. It was a strange and uncomfortable interaction, more than likely because neither of us knew how to relate to one another. I remember I had been peeling grapes when he came in and he looked at me inquisitively. We didn't have much to say to one another. One of the side effects of chemotherapy is that not only does the drug wipe out the bad chemo cells, but it also knocks out the good cells too. So there is a time frame of a couple of weeks with each cycle of chemo that I had very-little-to-no white blood cells. The primary function of a white blood cell is to fight off infections. Because of this, I was told that I could not eat the skin of fruits and vegetables. But I was craving grapes, so my friends would bring me in the biggest grapes they could find and I would sit there and peel them. I mean, I had the time. I looked up at my dad as I processed what he may have been thinking as he watched me peel each individual grape in silence, and all I said to him was, "I never did this before I came in here." As if to say, "I know this looks as weird as anything but don't worry, I'm good." I don't remember much else. My dad had seen the call of cancer as an opportunity for him to show up and try to be a father, and he did ... except that when he got to my room, he really didn't know how to do that and I was too sick to teach him. He showed up twice and then he was gone again.

I know my father was doing his best and I fully honour his desire to be supportive. It must be terribly difficult to have a child balancing between life and death and at the same time to be full of regrets and remorse over what could have or should have been. There were a few bright moments in my relationship with my father, a few acts of kindness on both our parts that seemed to auger well for a future relationship. But much as we both might have wanted the kind of unity a strong family relationship can provide, we just couldn't bridge the gap between us. My heart goes out to parents and their children everywhere who face a similar disconnect, and my hope for humanity is that someday these situations will be scarce.

It amazes me to look back at that time and see how the Universe allowed me the time and space to have a few private moments with both my father and my brother. Despite the fact that their visits had been unwelcome, they became moments of clarity and honest expression that would ultimately become a part of my healing journey. As I have shared, versions of this happened to me a couple of times, and I finally posted a sign on my door that said, "No Family Visitors." Now I know some may think this was harsh, but for me, it was about survival.

I needed to take the fastest route to protect my privacy and well-being. I felt scared and I was worried these uninvited, unannounced, and unwanted visitors were going to interfere with my recovery. I have learned that peace of mind is a huge component of the healing process and that is something this type of visitor does not support.

Just after my father left, I entered the non-stop nausea and vomiting phase of chemotherapy treatment and there was no communicating with anybody on any level. It was horrible. Despite the bucket loads of prophylactic anti-nausea medication given prior to the administration of a chemotherapy drug—and during it—I vomited continuously. During my second round of chemo, I ran into the lady who had been my PMH roommate in the out-patient chemo clinic. While Karen and I were both sitting in our chemo recliners, the subject of my nausea came up in our conversation. I remember saying to her that there was no rhyme, reason or pattern to my nausea and vomiting. And she immediately said, "Yes there was. It was ALL the time." And we both laughed.

Nothing the nurses administered to me gave me any relief and I was in agony. It was during this window of time that I believe my body went into self-preservation mode. You know how you hear people share stories of how something painful had happened to them—where the pain was so unbearable that they experienced short term memory loss or completely checked out? Well, I completely checked out. I believe that whatever was balled up in the mass that was now dissolving and disintegrating from the chemotherapy was now unleashed, and exposed. The pain, agony, suffering, and anger that had been collecting up inside me since those years of childhood neglect and abuse had crystallized into the baseball-sized tumour that had been threatening to stop my heart. As the chemotherapy dissolved the walls that held the tumour together, all of those negative emotions were freed from their prison. For a time, they circulated freely within my body. Because the shared goal of the mind and the body is survival, together they decided the best thing for me during this disintegration process was to protect me from the impact of the emotions in the tumour. Which is why I believe I checked out mentally.

I have no recollection of anything that happened over the course of several days. It was hard for me to think about that time, and it was hard for my dear friends to talk about it. Here is what Kerri had to say about that time:

"I remember there was a child-like vulnerability about you. Sometimes, you would sit up in bed when a wave of nausea would hit, with a pleading look in your eyes. I knew you were suffering physically but I could also sense your fear. You would cry and as you did, I would stroke your back from behind trying not to let you see that I was holding back tears.

This was a side of you I had never seen because you were only beginning to let your guard down in recovery. You had to be tough in your youth; you had your guard up against the world...

But as the chemo progressed, I witnessed you tap into your spirituality, and develop a quiet resolve to bear the challenge you were given... You had Faith that you were meant to live.

You would sleep an exhausted sleep but you weren't going to give in. You asked for help and it was there, but most of all I think you fed on the love that was around you."

Well if that doesn't make a person well up with emotion! I am so grateful to have Kerri in my life.

I don't clearly remember emerging back to wakefulness and awareness. I imagine that there was intense conflict going on between the emotions that were surfacing as the layers of the mass disintegrated. I believe the tumour contained knowledge, information, and feelings that were unacceptable to me, memories and feelings of which I wanted no part. It was all so intensely painful that it forced my mind to disconnect from my body, to protect me. Once my mind and body were both present again, and nausea and vomiting subsided, I settled into being a cancer patient.

There is one thing I will never forget and that is the odiferous chemo smell that oozed out of every cell and pore of my body. YUCK! I can almost smell it now as I think about it, and I have a visceral reaction that makes me scrunch up my face. The smell was so strong and powerful that it held me captive in the experience of illness. It is the smell of sickness, mixed with the toxic odor of *death*, with a sprinkle of uncertainty. As many brave souls before me, all those who go through chemotherapy treatment have no guarantee it will work, and because there are no other options, as was the case for me, we have no choice but to take on the uncertainty of it all. Cancer and uncertainty go hand in hand. We all learn to live with it, and the truth is, it never leaves you.

The Question to Ask Yourself:
Is there an aspect of my life where I should step into my discomfort and choose the tough option?

11

It's All About the Hair. More Complications

The next part of my journey seemed to be all about the hair. I learned it was not easy to be bald. The fact I had been blessed with beautiful hair and that I was a little too attached to it probably did not help. There is a timeline for hair loss in the cancer treatment world. At PMH, the nurse comes in on Day 10 like clock-work and says, "Are you ready for your head to be shaved?" This saves you from the long drawn out misery of watching your hair just start falling out all over the place on its own. It's tidier to have your head shaved. And, once that's taken care of, you don't have to worry about it all the time. In my case, in accordance with divine timing, as usual, my friend Kelly had dropped in for another visit the day I was scheduled for shaving, and I was not alone. I sat in a chair beside my bed while the nurse went to work on my head. I was a willing participant, and I was smiling and cooperative.

Afterward, I sat there and said nothing. The nurse asked if I would like to have a look and motioned towards the mirror in the bathroom. I nodded and with some trepidation, I stood up, took the few steps to the bathroom, and took one quick glance in the mirror. That's all I could handle. It was horrifying and painful to see my bald head for the first time and I ran the few steps back to my bed. I buried my face in my hands and sobbed. Losing the hair that I loved so much—that symbolized beauty to me—was really hard. Now what I saw in the mirror was a bald-headed cancer woman. I saw sickness reflected back at me, and it felt more real than ever in this moment of loss. Now I had complete confirmation that I was living as a cancer patient; I looked like one. Gone was my beautiful hair and in its place was sickness. So there I sat, weak and weary in every way, and tasked with processing the loss of my hair.

The first round of chemotherapy had been a traumatic

experience for me physically, mentally, and emotionally. As happens to some, I was that random person who seemed to suffer from more complications than normal, which made the recovery longer than usual and a little more miserable. I ended up getting infections in my blood, a small bowel obstruction, blood clots in my arm, and myriad other minor ailments. If there was a complication, I got it. My body was beaten up and battered and I needed my blood to replenish itself. Not unlike many cancer patients who have trudged this road before me, I had a long, tough road to recovery ahead.

I was now into week eight of my hospitalization, and I think because of the added complications I had come across, my future was feeling unclear, and fear was beginning to creep back. My body was having an extra hard time fighting off the infections in my blood and my temperature continued to spike; my heart was still beating too fast. The physicians had tried to put me on a heart medication called a beta-blocker twice in order to bring my heart rate down. My poor little heart. First, it had to endure living with a tumour that suffocated it and now it was stuck beating too fast and working too hard in response to all the work going on in my body. I strongly advocated for myself and twice I had refused the medication. The last thing I needed was to leave the hospital on heart medication. I was still on antibiotics for the fevers I had been experiencing. And I was feeling quite weak, and having trouble getting my strength back.

My body had been through a war and was still recovering from all it had been through. We were in the home stretch, we just didn't know it yet.

I was mentally drained from all that had happened. I was emotionally spent, as this ride I was on, was a lot to process. At this point, I really didn't know what I felt. I was also not as spiritually aligned as I needed to be and I was feeling that, too. I had not been to any AA meetings for some time, although the members of my home group brought a meeting to me in my hospital room once. I hadn't been meditating, and although I was still praying, it was not enough to keep me connected. I had spent two months as an inpatient at three different hospitals, and my discharge had had to be pushed back twice. It was still unclear whether or not the evil monster—the tumour—was still in my chest. On top of it all, I was feeling the effects of being too unwell to engage in my daily LiveWell Recipe. It was at this time of my life—where I was the weakest and weariest I'd ever been—that the strangest, most amazing thing happened. I am glad that, yet again, Kelly was with me at the time, or nobody would believe this part of my story.

"You Can Go Home Now"

Kelly and I were sitting comfortably together passing the time in my hospital room when the chief physician of the Malignant Hematology Unit nonchalantly strolled into my room. Kelly and I knew him well by this point, but we were completely thunderstruck when he said, "You can go home now. The mass is gone and the infection in your blood is clear." All I remember is thinking WHAT DO YOU MEAN THE MASS IS GONE? He then went on to tell us that only once in his career had he ever seen a case like this, and it had been in his residency, decades ago. He said my case represented a miracle. CT scans had been taken the previous day to look into my continued fevers and, also, to check for infections. The results were back. They showed no mass and no evidence of any infections whatsoever. In fact, the doctor shared the news that the radiologist working with him had been completely unable to locate the mass on the scan. He had had to check my previous CT scan to determine where he was supposed to be looking for it. The mass was gone, and there were no new abnormalities noted. "No abnormalities noted" is what you want to see written on a CT scan report.

I sat and listened to him in shock. I had a clean and clear CT scan for the first time since this nightmare had started.

It was almost surreal. After all, I had been through up until this point, and the slow pace of improvement. The nausea, the chills, the anxiety, the hair loss, the uncertainty, the struggles my body had been up against even during the last two weeks as it fought an uphill battle to bounce back from all that it had faced. Just like that, it was over. I would be discharged the next day. I could go home. It sounds easy, simple and exciting, but it certainly was not. I was physically exhausted and I certainly was not psychologically prepared for the about-face in my prognosis.

Life develops a rhythm in a hospital. You get used to the routines and the schedules, the medical visits, the tests, the checks, the medication, the company, and even the noises. To suddenly learn I was going to be discharged home the following day made me feel quite anxious and, to be honest, aside from the fear of going home alone, and out of the safe zone the hospital had provided for me, I was also in a panic about the fact that I was bald. I was afraid to face the world without my hair and at this point in the journey, I couldn't even entertain the idea of doing so. Going home without a wig at this point was not an option. It was an incredibly overwhelming experience. The idea that the mass was gone and I was going home, was crazy. Part of me wasn't sure if I believed that the mass was gone, afraid that it wasn't true, and I was fearful of what going home as "Cancer Tina" would be like for me. I was distressed by the shift from hospital to home and I did not feel prepared.

Because I was so filled with fear, I couldn't even enjoy the fact that I may have just beaten cancer. I mean, how amazing is that?! At least, it should have been. But I couldn't even begin to process that yet. It was the strangest thing. I was so afraid to go home, that I arranged with my physician to let me stay one more day. I was so full of fears around going home that I wanted to postpone it, crazy as that may sound. I had told my doctor that I had arrangements to take care of before I could leave. In fact, all the arrangements were really about sorting out in my own mind that I was going home…and allowing me to begin to process all of what that would mean.

The next morning Kelly took me wig shopping. It's one of those things you just don't think you would ever do … never say never certainly applies here. Well, I have to say that it didn't take long at all to choose new hair: There it was, literally the first wig I saw. I took off the little knit cap the hospital had given me and the store assistant helped me place the grip band on my head. Then she placed the wig on me. It was unbelievable how closely this wig resembled my own hair: it was the exact colour, consistency, and style as mine, although it was a little shorter. Kelly had been seeing me bald for the better part of a month, so when I turned around and looked at her, she cried. I turned and looked in the mirror and then I cried, too. It was a profound and powerful experience for both of us. Kelly dropped me back off at the hospital where I would spend my last night as an inpatient at PMH.

The next morning I sat on my hospital bed filled with trepidation as I waited for a friend to pick me up and take me home. It's really hard to explain what I was feeling that morning, and all I know is I did not feel ready to go home. I was full of fear, and something didn't feel right. Countless thoughts about the events of the past eight weeks zig-zagged through my head and the emotions coursing through me were intense and scattered. Part of me wanted to jump for joy and holler from the rooftops, but the strangeness of what I was feeling held me back. I was happy and relieved to be leaving Princess Margaret Hospital and I had already postponed my discharge by a day. So, why didn't I want to go? I think now that it's partly because I was uncomfortable stepping out into the world wearing a wig to hide my baldness, with an overly thin body and ill-fitting clothes. I had lost a total of 23 pounds and it showed on my 5'7" frame. Maybe I was afraid because I lived alone in my condo, and I didn't want to be alone. Maybe it was because somehow I knew there was a tough road still ahead for me. Maybe I just wasn't processing how close to death I had actually come?

In the end, I pushed through the fear and put one foot in front of the other. I put on a brave face along with my beautiful new wig. I stepped out into the land of the living.

The Question to Ask Yourself:
How do I define beauty in myself? And in others?

12

More Chemo

The first morning after being discharged from the hospital I woke up unsure of my surroundings. It seemed eerily quiet in comparison to the noise and hustle-bustle I had been accustomed to at the hospital. I lay there still for a moment as I took stock of where I actually was and how I was feeling. I remember feeling a little excited about the freedom of being out of the hospital, but, more than anything I was focused on the fact that even though I was well enough to be discharged, I wasn't feeling very well. I knew I had to keep moving, though, and I realized some sunlight would do me good. I shuffled around and I put on my wig and a sweater. I am sure many others who have been really sick can relate to the fact that posture and mobility are affected by illness. Even though I had lost weight, it felt like my limbs were too heavy for what little strength I had and I wasn't able to lift and move them as I normally would. I slowly made my way to the elevator on my floor, shuffling my legs along in an effort to appear to be the version of Tina I had been before the cancer. I held my head high and made my way slowly down to the ground floor After what seemed like forever, I passed through the glass doors of my building and stood on the sidewalk outside. I was grateful it was a glorious sunny day but what I was feeling was anything but glorious. In my first moment outside, I felt the warmth of the sun as it beat down on me, and in the second moment, all I could do was cry. It was an outpour of emotion that I could not hold back. I'm sure I must have looked like a frightened child or a deer in the headlights of an oncoming car, as fear radiated from my eyes to the world around me and the tears just flowed and flowed.

I returned back inside, a little embarrassed by my outpouring of emotion, and exhausted by the effort it had taken me to leave my condo.

I was a little perplexed the next day when I woke up feeling a little worse than I had the first morning. My physical state worsened as the day progressed, and on into the next day I was still feeling more miserable. It didn't make any sense to me. What I didn't know at the time of discharge was that I had a very bad case of "Red Man Syndrome" brewing inside my already weak and frail body. Red Man Syndrome is an adverse reaction to an antibiotic and it is characterized by redness, swelling, burning, and pruritus—itching. I went to bed only to be awakened in the middle of the night by a burning sensation in both of my hands. It felt as though I had whacked them on a hard, cold, steel wall. The rest of the night I tossed and turned and the following morning I was worse again.

I lay down on my couch looking at the fridge but feeling incapable of getting up to make something to eat. I was also delaying getting up to go to the bathroom because the task seemed so daunting.

I became so sick and weak that I realized I could not manage on my own; I needed help. I felt bad bothering Kerri and Brock again, as they had just picked me up from the hospital three days earlier to bring me home and they had done so much for me already. But I couldn't do this alone and I knew I wasn't in good shape. I texted them both and said I could barely get to the fridge, let alone stand long enough to prepare a meal. Could they please bring me some meal replacement drinks? Brock came that day with Ensure beverages. I was so grateful.

Asking for help that day—when I thought I should have been able to make it on my own—marked the beginning of me learning to have a voice, one that expressed my needs and didn't let pride get in the way. I lived alone and I was really sick. I realized that I needed help in all kinds of ways and to make it through this phase of my journey I had to start speaking up and asking. For my fear, I needed connection and moral support. For my weakness, I needed help with my meals and chores. And, for my loneliness, I needed some company and some love.

I was grateful that I had been teaching yoga for many years in the condo complex where I lived, and I had a roster of students and their contact information to draw on. I had built relationships with a number of my students, and many of them knew that I had stopped teaching due to illness. They were all kind-hearted people. Perhaps some of them might be able to assist? The first yoga student I reached out to for help in my fear and desperation had known very little about my illness and how sick I actually was. Lucky for me, she answered her phone and came right over. The look on her face when she arrived at my condo and saw the state I was in was one of shock, concern, and care. It was not at all surprising, as this was her first time meeting Cancer Patient Tina. Bless her heart, she must have sensed exactly what I needed and, on the spot, she offered to run back to her place and grab an overnight bag so she could spend the night with me at my condo. She didn't want me to be alone. I will never forget how much comfort I took just knowing someone else was there. She stayed with me that night, during which time my symptoms worsened. The tingling and burning that had started out in my hands had now progressed to include my feet, and face. The pain was increasing and these body parts began to swell. I came close to calling 911, but I had to weigh which scenario would be worse; to wait this through and hope to be okay, or to go through the humiliating experience of having Emergency Medical Services (EMS) take me through my lobby and back to the hospital. I made it through that night, and the following morning another yoga student graciously took me to my appointment with my oncologist, Dr. Schuh, at PMH.

The Horrors of Red Man Syndrome

When I got there I lay in agony on a stretcher in a sickbay. I can still conjure up the memory of myself that day and it wasn't pretty. I was wearing my wig because I was still self-conscious about being bald, and I had been barely able to pull my boots on over my swollen feet. I lay on the stretcher with my arms extended out to the side, palms facing up, and my legs were bent in a bit to accommodate my boots as the heels dug into the stretcher. My face was red and visibly bloated, as though I had a really nasty sunburn. I felt embarrassed about how I looked and even today the memories of that day make me feel uncomfortable. This day, in particular, was as vivid and clear as if it were yesterday. I can see Dr. Schuh standing at the foot of my stretcher and the look on his face confirmed just how bad I looked.

This agonizing memory reminds me of what all cancer patients experience, in their own way, as they make their way through the illness; each person pushes through extreme amounts of discomfort—physically, mentally, and emotionally—and there are uncomfortable complications. The cancer journey is certainly a testament to the strength of the human spirit.

The first words out of Dr. Schuh's mouth were, "You are a mess." He then went on to say that I had Red Man Syndrome and that he had only seen one other case that was as bad as mine. He explained that I was essentially burning from the inside out due to a severe and rare allergic reaction to the antibiotic Vancomycin. To sum this part up is easy; it was BRUTAL. You know you are badly burned if the palms of your hands and the soles of your feet are affected. Rarely do they peel. And that is exactly what happened. I had the bizarre experience of watching the skin on the soles of my feet and the palms of my hands begin to peel very thick layers. It was kind of like a moccasin peeled off of each foot. Even though I had been alerted to the fact that this was going to happen, it was a shocking sight, which is basically what my friend Kerri said when she came over to see me after I returned home the next day. What followed were days of sweeping as I shed from head to toe, just like a snake.

It was actually Halloween when this happened and I sent a picture of my hands to a few friends who thought the hands had been manufactured as part of some scary costume. They had no idea that the "fake" Halloween hands were actually mine.

However painful and difficult the Red Man Syndrome was, some good did come out of the experience; it served as another prompt to help me learn to access my voice and to use it. I was beginning to speak the language of self-care, and I now found myself saying things like, "that doesn't work for me," "I can't do this," and "I need help." These were things I had never felt very comfortable saying before, as pride—one of the seven deadly sins—had always gotten in my way. I had previously preferred to remain in a state of discomfort rather than say I couldn't do something, or burden other people with a request. As humans, we sometimes become conditioned to just managing things on our own, and at times our pride blocks us from asking for help when we need it. Sometimes people find it easier to accept the status quo, as it seems like too much effort to express a preference and make a change. And sometimes change is just scary and we back away from acting or living any differently than we are used to. Sometimes we do not even realize we have learned to behave in a way that does not allow us to use our voice.

As a child, it had been normal for me to not use my voice at all. I just acted like I was okay, even if I were in discomfort. I spent most of my life in discomfort, in fact—it was a state that actually became normal for me when I had been a young girl. Many of us, and particularly women, suffer in silence. We remain in discomfort despite the fact that there is help around us if we would only ask.

The other side of this is that when we decide not to ask we are also denying those who love and care about us an opportunity to connect and be there for us in a way that might give them purpose and soul work. Underneath it all, I believe we are all wired this way. Today, I am much more able to ask for help and I enjoy feeling comforted when I allow people to help me when I am in need.

After the Red Man Syndrome had mostly cleared up. I was back for another appointment with Dr. Schuh so he could assess whether or not I was ready to start my second of three rounds of chemotherapy. It may seem strange that the tumour was gone and yet I was still scheduled to undergo more chemotherapy, but cancer and how it is treated is unlike any other area of medicine. There is a focus on being extra-certain each and every malicious cell has indeed been removed. Up next, round two. My red blood cell, white blood cell, and platelet counts were normal, and, therefore, in good shape for starting the second round of chemotherapy. But my hands had not yet healed from the Red Man Syndrome. In fact, they were still cracked, split and raw, even weeping in some areas. This could represent a major source of potential infection for a chemotherapy patient. And of most concern to me was that I knew this would delay my self-imposed timeline for finishing treatment. I felt my extended stay in the hospital, required to deal with complications during my first round of chemotherapy, had put me behind schedule. In essence, I felt behind on the timeline to save my life. I felt anxious and fearful and I was eager to move ahead. Kelly came with me to my appointment that day, and she knew I was determined to start the next round of chemo the following week.

Dr. Schuh took one look at my hands, and said, "You won't be ready to start chemo next week with hands like that." I was devastated. I begged and pleaded with him, but he looked at me and shook his head. Both Dr. Schuh and Kelly were united in the conviction that there was no way my hands would be healed in time for chemo and, truth to tell, it did look highly unlikely. Bless Dr. Schuh's heart, though, because despite the evidence my hands presented to him, he humoured me. He told me to come back the following Monday and, if my hands were healed enough by then, he would be willing to go ahead and start treatment on Tuesday. Otherwise, I was going to have to wait another week. We were already sitting at Wednesday, which meant my body had five days to heal. This was to become the second miracle Kelly would witness in my health. My levels of motivation and determination were off the charts as I nursed my hands around the clock for the next five days, leaning on my Higher Power to assist.

My nursing skills would prove to be helpful as I did meticulous wound care once every afternoon, and again during the middle of the night. I needed sleeping pills and narcotics to fall asleep because I was still feeling the burning effects of the Red Man Syndrome, so when I would awaken in the middle of the night I would immediately take my next round of pills to both alleviate my pain and help me fall back asleep. While I waited for the medication to take effect, I would tend to my hands. I turned my bathroom floor into a mini-wound-care bay as it provided the light and space I needed, and I set up my supplies there for easy access: gauze, sterile saline, scissors, clean towels, Q-tips and antibiotic ointment. I would spend countless hours debriding the wounds on my hands and my feet. I made endless gentle dabs with dry gauze, and countless snips with tiny scissors in hopes that I would speed up the healing process to be ready to start my next round of chemo. I did not want to wait another week! Honestly, I know it is hard to believe, but by Monday morning I had done it. My hands were ready. My Higher Power and I had created a miracle. The chemotherapy went ahead. This triumphant little story still makes me smile today!

Groundhog Day (Maybe)

The second and third rounds of chemo were administered to me on an out-patient basis at PMH and trips to this hospital became the template for my life. It felt like I was always there for chemotherapy treatments, follow up appointments, blood work, blood transfusions, and a myriad of other tests. During this time I lived a "Groundhog Day" life as a cancer patient, where it felt as though every day was exactly like the one before it but, honestly, this was a good thing, because that is all I had the energy for. I was experiencing a lot of fatigue and I didn't have much time or energy for anything besides my hospital routine and my daily LiveWell Recipe. In my efforts to have some normalcy, I resumed teaching the weekly yoga classes in my condo building that I had started before my life had been hijacked by cancer. A dangling IV line—called a Picc line— had to stay embedded in my right arm until chemo was over, so I covered it with a pretty knit arm warmer, and covered my bald head with a knit cap, and away I went. As for the wig, I never really warmed up to it and I had broken up with it soon after my second round of chemo started. As much as I could initially not fathom facing the world with no hair, the truth was, it was easier to face the world bald, with a little knit cap, as Cancer Patient Tina, than to wear a wig and pretend to be okay when I wasn't. I had the cutest little knit cap that my friend Kristina had knitted for me and it helped a lot. I recently looked at a picture of me wearing that wig and it really did look pretty good ... it just didn't feel good. To live in truth is a comfortable place for me, and hiding the fact that I was sick and bald just did not feel right. I was immensely grateful that I quickly evolved and grew to a place where self-esteem issues around the baldness no longer mattered. I found a place of self-acceptance, and I became comfortable facing the world as I was. And the truth was, I was Cancer Patient Tina and I had no hair.

During this time I also took on a volunteer yoga position that had come up at the Centre for Addiction and Mental Health (CAMH). The timing might not have seemed perfect, but I realized that if I didn't apply for it right then and there, I would have to wait another year, as this was a year- long posting. There was no way I was going to wait another year for this opportunity—it was perfect for me—so I went for it. I think that in some ways this was another way for me to say out loud to the world that I was not going anywhere, that I was going to live, and that productive work felt right and good. I wore my wig to the interview because I did not want my potential employer to know that I was in the middle of fighting cancer and I was thrilled when I was offered the position. The orientation process was a little uncomfortable but I stuck it out, and I am so glad I did. It was welcomed work that filled my soul, and now, more than six years later I still retain that volunteer position and I am grateful to have it. Clients are always so appreciative of the classes I teach for them, but truthfully … little do they know how much they are helping me.

During the three months of the second and third rounds of chemo, I did pretty well. My chemotherapy treatment did consume a lot of my time, but I also worked hard at implementing as much of my LiveWell Recipe as possible. My world was almost all about self-care, in part because it had to be, but even more because before I ever got sick, self-care had been a big part of my everyday life. I went to as many AA meetings as I could physically manage and I would sit in the far back corner, away from everybody, to be as safe as I could be. At times I had no white blood cells to fight off infections. The chemotherapy I was getting would knock my cell counts right down to zero. It really is crazy amazing what the body can withstand and how it can bounce back from enormous peril. I also started to go into my clinical psychologist's office for my sessions with her, which was also good for me. For a time I had been too sick to go anywhere, and my sessions up until this point had taken place over the phone from my bed at home.

I spent a lot of time alone during this part of the journey and I am blessed to have had the time to be with myself, to heal on so many levels. I had no partner, I lived alone, and I continued to be estranged from old friends from my hometown, and from my family. Aside from visits from a small circle of good friends, I spent numerous hours by myself during the long, frigid winter of 2013. The amazing thing was that I did not feel alone. When I look back at this time, I can honestly say I felt some form of a presence with me much of the time. I felt a foreign kind of comfort in and around me. I distinctly remember hanging up the phone after a call with my clinical psychologist one day and saying to myself, "Am I really this okay with all this?" I lay comfortably propped up on the pillows in my bed. How could I possibly be okay? But I was. Whatever this presence or energy that was with me was, it gave me a form of complete comfort. My last round of chemo went off pretty much without a hitch, except for one complication that could be traced back to me forgetting to take the anti-inflammatory eye drops regularly. I woke up two days post treatment with my eyes burning as if citrus had been splashed in my eyes. The result was that my vision was damaged. And I had to get new prescription eyeglasses. My last round of chemo ended December 23rd and the next stage of my cancer journey began.

The Questions to Ask Yourself:
Do I have a voice?
Am I able to speak up and ask for help when I need it or do I let pride get in the way?

13

Debilitating Fatigue and Heightened Senses

It was a new year, I was tumour-free, and my chemotherapy was complete. I wanted to be a true survivor, and to me, that meant freeing myself of the role of "cancer victim" as soon as possible. I was on a mission to fight my way back to my pre-cancerous state. My mood was beginning to elevate, and I was starting to get excited about my life again. But what I didn't know was that the real hard work of recovery was about to begin. There was to be no jumping back into life like I had wanted; I had thought that my energy would start improving, but I was wrong. My illness had its own timeline. I would come to learn the fatigue I had experienced throughout the entire four months of the chemotherapy phase of my journey, was nothing compared to what lay ahead.

As a nurse, I had learned from my studies and my work how amazing the human body is, but as a patient, I would learn how intelligent and accommodating that body could be. First, I must say that I am not a medical doctor and I can only report what I felt and experienced. It is really hard to explain it, but it was almost as if during the entire chemotherapy treatment, my body was idling in neutral as if it were just operating enough so it would not stall. It was permitting the chemotherapy to take centre stage and do its work to save my life. As soon as the last of the chemotherapeutic drug had left my system, my body came back online with a vengeance. The surprising thing was that it did not come back as I would have expected, with increased or renewed energy. Instead, its comeback was marked by debilitating fatigue and hypersensitivity. I had no clue this was going to happen, as nobody had warned me. It would have been nice to know this, although we all know there is no rulebook for cancer. This was my journey, and my version of cancer and, as many others before me had done, I forged ahead and pushed through.

It was the craziest thing; it was as if all of my senses had been turned way down during the chemo and now, without warning, they were turned back on, and dialed up to the max, leaving me in a vastly heightened state of awareness. Sounds were louder, lights were brighter and I became acutely sensitive to temperature. I found myself backing away from people a little to give myself more physical space. I moved away from speakers because they were too loud. I had to get to know my body's limits again and it was kind of freaky. I dimmed the lights and I wore extra sweaters. It was so intense, that I felt overwhelmed when I was out in public in uncontrolled environments. I spoke with a yoga teacher about what I was experiencing and he said: "Tina, when you try to put a sweater on a baby, they don't just get fussy because they want to be difficult, it is because it is just too much, too fast for them to handle." This explanation made so much sense to me; like a baby, I was experiencing too much of everything too fast. As I went through what I now call my hypersensitive phase, I realized loud noises, extreme temperatures and bright lights are a major stress on anyone's body, not just mine. The work involved in adjusting to changes in the wavelengths of light, constantly filtering out the stress of noise, and ensuring correct thermoregulation of the body to maintain a normal temperature is constant and ongoing.

These autoregulatory mechanisms that most of us take for granted can drain our energy stores. We don't even realize the work our bodies have to do to constantly recalibrate, adjust, filter and regulate our systems in order to find and feel balance, harmony, and comfort. I see this daily in my work as an ICU nurse. During my shift I need to be constantly filtering out, sifting through, and processing an endless onslaught of bings, bongs, and bells that are produced by the monitors and life-saving equipment around me. It can be exhausting. I have especially noticed the impact of noise on the days I teach yoga after I have worked a 12-hour shift in the ICU. To go directly from spending 12 hours working in the chaotic noise of the

ICU, to teaching a yoga class in a silent auditorium sets up an interesting contrast. I can literally feel the soft calm settling into and onto my physical body as I sit in silence. It is a healthy and beautiful thing.

Hungry, Angry, Lonely, Tired ... and Cold

As I mentioned, the LiveWell Recipe that I created and used to help me with my sobriety became immensely helpful in cancer recovery as well. Remember the acronym HALT plus Cold that I talked about previously? It was a blessing to have the awareness and understanding of HALT to apply and use in this hypersensitivity phase of my cancer recovery. I followed my HALT + Cold protocol and I took it to another level based on an even larger awareness of how important it was to adjust the external environment in order to feel comfortable and avoid discomfort. In short, I become even more aware of my surroundings and I took notice of what doesn't feel good. Whenever possible, I make adjustments. And I continue to pack snacks in case I get hungry, and a sweater in case I feel cold, just as I initially learned to do when I first implemented HALT in my recovery from alcoholism, and just as I did as I was recovering from cancer. The protocol works no matter what's going on in my life or how much I need to recalibrate my existence because I am really removing variables of discomfort.

Fatigue was a major aspect of my healing process that I hadn't expected. I had been tired all the time during all three rounds of chemotherapy, but nothing like what hit me once it was finished. It was different. It felt as if I was unplugged from my energy source as if I were a drained battery. It wasn't the kind of fatigue that became progressively worse as the day went on; I would just wake up each and every day in extreme fatigue. My heart goes out to the women of the world who have to care for little ones while battling cancer and dealing with this extreme level of fatigue. I found myself feeling grateful that I didn't have any children at home. I, personally, found I had to stagger my activities, allowing myself only one main task or chore per day. If I had a follow-up appointment at PMH, I would not add any other tasks into that day. It took more than six months for the fatigue to lift and it seemed like it went on forever. Bit by bit, it finally left me. And because it lasted so long, I began to associate fatigue with being sick. I had a mind-body-fear connection wired into me, and even a couple of years after the illness ended, fatigue would still evoke a fear response in me. I would still worry when I became fatigued that I was starting to get sick again. These would become moments in my life where I would have to find strength in my faith and choose to just not let fear in.

During this time I had no choice but to accept the slow, incremental healing as I progressively regained my strength and my physical capabilities. The days were long and the healing process was slow but, for the most part, I felt peaceful and calm. Netflix, my new "lover" helped a lot and I don't think my convalescence would have been complete without it. I continued to wake up in deep gratitude because almost anything was better than the tough and dark days I had experienced at Princess Margaret Hospital. In the worst of those dark, gloomy days, I would wake up to the toxic smell of chemo, and the first order of business would be to get through the vomiting, nosebleeds, body aches, and diarrhea. There were mornings when I would wake up knowing I might not make it to the toilet and as I sat barely holding myself up, I would turn and vomit into the garbage can. Then, while I sat as upright as my strength would allow, with my head still hanging between my legs, I would feel the wetness of blood dripping from a fresh nosebleed onto my bare legs. As I wiped the chemo smelling blood from my nose, I would think to myself, "Well, it doesn't get much worse than this." I would shuffle back to bed where I would lie waiting for a better moment ahead. Those were dark, scary, painful mornings that I would not wish on anyone. I mean, how could I not feel anything but gratitude now that I had cleared the hurdle of cancer treatment? Yet for months and months, I would wake up and for a flash of a second, I would think I was back at PMH, and my breath would stop. Then I would flash to another moment, the present-day moment, but I would have to walk my mind out. "Oh, I am okay and alive again today. I am not in pain, I am not lying in a bed at PMH, and I am not in that dark place anymore. Thank you, God."

It is kind of like when you wake up on a Saturday morning and for that brief moment you think you have to get up to go to work, and then you realize it's the weekend. And you are like, "N-i-c-e! It's Saturday and I don't have to get up or go to work today." The up-side to waking up to a flash of post- traumatic stress disorder (PTSD) was that each day started in deep gratitude and a strong sense of spirituality. And sometimes, once the PTSD moment had passed, I just woke up excited to be alive. I have to tell you, to wake up in this kind of gratitude as your default setting is a gift. It makes so much sense to me now why so many people start out their day by making a gratitude list. I loved those mornings when I would wake up in gratitude, and I cherish the memories today.

Reliance on my LiveWell Recipe based primarily on self-care undoubtedly helped me through the process. I had to be patient with myself and accept that my body was not as it had been before. I was physically weak. I took baby steps and worked very hard, with great determination, to get my strength, my health, and my life back. I took my recovery very seriously and I looked at it as my responsibility to make this happen; I put forth all my effort at all times. I started each day with prayer and a healthy breakfast. You are what you eat is a cliché for a reason and, for obvious reasons health was my top priority. I would make sure that I engaged in exercise daily, either by doing yoga or by jogging on-the-spot in my living room. It was a frigid winter and I didn't dare to go outside very much. I was teaching weekly yoga classes and I had sessions with my clinical psychologist twice a week. I also attended AA meetings twice a week. Add in my PMH appointments, and

I kept pretty busy. For the most part, I was able to embrace this part of the process. I just kept putting one foot in front of the other. And I believe that the reason I managed to do this on a daily basis despite difficulties was because I believed that life was bigger than myself and I stayed connected to God. It was through this connection, that I received the strength that I needed to keep moving forward.

Are You the Patient?

I had many follow up appointments in the Hematology clinic at PMH but there is one appointment that further inspired me and reinforced for me the fact that my LiveWell Recipe was really working for me. On this particular day, I walked into the waiting room as usual and walked up to the receptionist for my routine check-in. My hair had grown back enough to seem as though it might be a specific style statement and I went through the checklist of things patients are asked to do like clockwork each time they arrive: sign in, fill out the standard health-related questionnaire and hop up on the scale. After I had completed all of the required tasks, I took my usual spot in the waiting room where I sat patiently for my name to be called. Unbeknownst to me, a lady had been watching me go through this process and once I was settled she came up to me and with some hesitation said, "Are you the patient?" I paused for a second as I looked at her, and then I smiled, sat up straight and with pride I said, "Yes, I am!" Her smiled was wrapped in awe and with admiration. "Good for you!" she said. I felt enormous gratitude in that moment as I reaped the benefits of all my hard work and my LiveWell Recipe. It felt to me as though this lady had just witnessed my inner spirit drive. In that moment I felt a strong connection to God, a strong connection to mankind, and on some level, I felt in control of my health for the first time in a long time.

Over time, my strength returned and my vital force gradually settled back into my body. I was starting to feel refreshed and very much alive. It is an incredible feeling to walk around and feel so lucky to be alive. There really is nothing like it. I can only describe it as similar to the feeling you may have when you find out you have succeeded at achieving something that you worked extremely hard for—a win that was more than well-deserved. Something that you put your heart, soul, and guts into. Something that, despite your efforts, you might *not* have won, and then, when you hear the news, you are elated, excited and, of course, grateful. Magnify that by the fact that your life is on the line, and that's what I was feeling. It was incredible.

The Question to Ask Yourself:
What is one thing my life that I am especially grateful for?

14

Continued Transformation

As I ran the electric razor over my scalp and looked into the mirror, I still couldn't believe what I saw. I held back tears while I finished shaving my head and then I sat on the floor and wept. I wept for the loss of my beautiful hair and I wept for all the pain I had endured as I had gone through my cancer nightmare. I also wept for everything I had gone through that had brought me to this point, and I felt waves of emotion from years past, as if the shedding of the hair also allowed for the shedding of some pain I no longer needed to carry.

After chemo, it takes some time for all of your hair follicles to start growing again so, in the beginning, your hair comes in patchy and sparse. For this reason, it is best to keep your head shaved. I will be honest; it was not easy for me to be a bald woman. I know some women choose to be bald and they are beautiful and can rock the style, but for me, it was the opposite. Because I did not choose to be bald, it symbolized cancer, and lustrous hair symbolized beauty. I missed my hair, and I missed my health. As my hair grew back my after-shower routine shifted from just wiping my scalp dry to having to wrap a towel around my head again. There is something very sensual about that act of wrapping a towel around your head and to me, it signified the return of health and beauty. In that beautiful moment, as I removed the towel I had wrapped on my head again for the first time, I sat on my bathroom floor and wept again. But that day, they were tears of gratitude. I felt, and still do feel happy, lucky, and grateful. As my hair grew back, I, also, grew into a new version of myself. I was forever changed from my cancer experience, and although difficult, I was grateful for the change. There is a larger meaning for me when somebody compliments me and says, "Your hair is beautiful." Forever now, that simple compliment will send a signal to my brain and open up the gates of gratitude. To lose something you love so much, and then to get it back again, is incredible. Every single day my hair reminds me that I am alive and that grace exists in my life. Winning the hair lottery for the second time was an added bonus.

Initially, I did harbour feelings of resentment and anger that I went through alcoholism alone and now here I was facing the challenge of cancer alone as well. Spending much of the time convalescing physically alone is not an ideal scenario for waging war on cancer. When I say alone, I specifically mean without a loving partner. Yes, there were times that were difficult and I wished that someone were there to comfort and nurture me, and help me with my struggles. But I can see now how beneficial it was for me to be alone. Being alone allowed me to focus on self-study and inner work and it took my healing to a whole other level. While I healed physically, mentally, and emotionally, I was able to evolve and grow in leaps and bounds. If I had had a partner, I would have been distracted and likely would not have achieved anywhere near as much growth from the experience. It was as if being alone to go through the cancer had put me on the fast track for personal healing and evolution. Now, don't get me wrong, it also required a lot of hard and uncomfortable work. But the transformation that occurred allowed me to get closer to the innate, authentic version of Tina.

Having had this amazing growth experience, I feel compelled to share that it is this exact reasoning we are advised to not date while in the first year of sobriety, or longer. The thing is this, as soon as you enter into an intimate relationship your healing and evolution towards your best self come to an abrupt halt because you are now distracted from the task of self-discovery. Early in sobriety, we also need to acknowledge and accept that we do not have the internal resources beyond working a program to manage the complexities of dating and all that goes along with it. From my experience I have come to learn that time spent alone on our journey is time for self-discovery and growth. And the truth is the better the version of yourself you evolve to, the better the partner you will end up connecting with. It's worth the wait. In the end, I was blessed to have had minimal distractions in both of my recoveries.

Living With Uncertainty

About six months into my cancer journey I showed up at PMH for one of my regularly-scheduled follow-up visits. The usual routine check-up included blood work, a meeting with the doctor, and then a CT scan. On this particular day, I got the blood work completed but when I met with Dr. Schuh he casually announced he was not ordering me a CT scan. A CT scan is a series of very detailed X-ray images that use computer technology to create pictures of your organs, bones, and other tissues.[20] He said that there were no signs the cancer had returned and that we were not going to go looking for it.

Okay. In hindsight, that makes perfect sense, but in that moment, I freaked out a little bit. I said, "WHAT...NO CT SCAN? WHY NOT?" I realized that I had come to like the certainty the CT scans gave me, as they were a conclusive way of telling me I was okay. The picture shows the evil guy has not returned. Dr. Schuh explained his rationale and I did understand, intellectually, but I still walked out of there in a state of panic. All I could think about was that I now had to wait three months until my next appointment to get concrete confirmation from a CT scan the mass had not returned.

The discomfort associated with the uncertainly was not easy to sit with. I had to work through all the thoughts that were running through my mind. I imagine people who have survived a very bad car accident have to push through their fears long after their physical injuries have healed in order to get back on the road again. I still, to this day, have flashes of

---

[20] WebMD, https://www.webmd.com/cancer/what-is-a-ct-scan, accessed November 4, 2019

fear that the mass may come back and I will die, although this happens less frequently now than previously. When these fears do arise, I pray. I now know that the only way to have emotional stability is to embrace my faith. Faith is the only thing that has power over uncertainty.

Living with fear and uncertainty was not new to me, as it has been a part of my life for some time now. The reality of living with alcoholism is that you have no *mental* defense against that first drink. I have also now learned that when living with cancer you have no *physical* defense against that first malicious cell sticking, and heralding the return of the cancer. The only defense I have against either is a spiritual one. In this time of great fear and uncertainty, I chose to trust, and I turned to my faith. I drew again on my LiveWell Recipe and put extra effort into the spiritual category—prayer, meditation, AA meetings, and doing things for other people. I take great comfort in knowing I am showing up in life with faith and I let the rest unfold as it will.

Becoming More Spiritually Connected

The start of my spiritual journey began in desperation when I was battling alcoholism and my life was on the line. One of the first things I was told to do at my inaugural AA meeting was to pray. I prayed and I stayed sober. This first step on what I now see to be my spiritual path led me to believing in a power greater than myself. I showed up with willingness and I put forth the effort to connect. I found by doing these simple things I began to feel a shift happening. Slowly, over time, my spiritual practice grew, and I was grateful to have a practice in place when I became sick with the cancer. It scares me now to think about what my cancer experience would have been like for me had I not had my faith. The funny thing was, when faced with the cancer, faith was all I had. And, as it turns out, faith is everything. Throughout my recovery, I continued to build upon the foundation I had already put in place. My practice deepened and I became even more spiritually connected. There were times, though, when it didn't make sense to me to be lying there in the middle of this cancer journey—alone, and bald, and feeling so calm, comfortable and content, but in those moments, I really was. What I didn't quite realize at the time, that I can see so clearly now, was that my personal relationship with a higher power—the God of my understanding and the strength of my spiritual belief—had become quite strong, and it was so present in my life that I could feel it.

I began to foster and grow a spiritual perspective on life, and I felt comforted, I began to seek more. I was comforted more. I had everything I needed to make it through, and I did. As I look back today at how my spiritual program came to be, it amazes me. It did not happen overnight, but rather it was a process and an evolution that required active participation. I did my spiritual work on a daily basis, and this left me open to being receptive to God. With the channels open, Grace flowed in. Life is much easier now that I am living in faith. I do my part, I show up and I turn it all over and let it unfold as it should. Today I still work to keep the channels open, by praying, meditating, attending AA meetings, doing things for other people and pursuing a life of self-study. And the grace of God flows in. I have noticed, if I do not practice the components of my spiritual regime on a regular basis, my day-to-day life seems to be a little more difficult. I notice I begin to feel as if I am wound up tighter, and this manifests as discomfort. I notice I become more reactive and less patient. I also believe I become less compassionate and understanding. Overall, I'm not at my best. I have come to see that if I am struggling with anything, big or small, it can often be traced back to the fact that I am not coming from a place of spiritual connectedness. If I begin to see or feel the shift in me, I immediately go to my spiritual practices to bring myself back into spiritual alignment. What's more, even though I have experienced the benefits of spiritual practice, and witnessed them in others, I sometimes still find myself straying from putting forth enough effort in this category. I am a continual work-in-progress.

Amazingly, but not surprisingly, I ultimately came to see that my spiritual evolution was closely linked to the evolution of my personal healing. As I grew spiritually, I healed emotionally. As I healed emotionally, I began to settle into the Tina I am today. I came to a place where I could face myself entirely and look myself in the mirror. I could look at myself as I was, without turning away. I could see all of myself, faults and all, with clarity, compassion, and understanding. I don't think I would have been able to do this without a spiritual connection. I can now look at who I had been in the past and feel less shame. When I was finally able to do this, I began to start to like Tina, the person I saw in the mirror. I became more accepting of what I was and what I wasn't, and it became much easier and more comfortable to be me. I had become connected on a deeper level with my intimate self, my spirit, and my soul. I started feeling my soul and its love for me.

About a year or so after chemo ended, I was fully recovered and back to work. I had a session with an aboriginal healer during which the issue of my cancer recovery came up. I shared with the healer that I felt some kind of presence or energy had carried me while I had been sick. The aboriginal healer's interpretation of this was that the presence I had felt was, in fact, the spirit of my mother. The Healer stated that she had been with me and that she had carried me. The disease of alcoholism did not allow my mother to be what I needed, while she was alive and I was growing up. During my formative years, she had not been able to give the nurturing that Tina as a little girl had so badly needed and wanted. Now, during this difficult time, she had come to help me. My mother's spirit and God's soul had created the mysterious blanket of warmth I had felt, and the energy that had carried me. With her spirit, she did what she was not able to do for me while she was alive. I like to believe this to be true, and I take great comfort in it. I am so grateful I had been that far on my spiritual journey, to have had the channels open and to be receptive, or I would not have had that wonderful experience while I was healing from cancer. Against the odds, I beat the Myeloid Sarcoma I had been faced with and came out the other side in a much better place mentally, spiritually, and emotionally. And, eventually, I was able to regain my pre-cancerous physical state as well. I didn't just take my life back, I took a better version back, so I most certainly can say that I am a grateful cancer survivor.

I have deep gratitude to have been given all that I needed to support and foster such a miraculous recovery. I realize how blessed I am to have come out on the other side of my personal cancer journey with a miraculous amount of healing, resilience, and gifts.

The Questions to Ask Yourself:
What can I do right now to start working through any pain I have been carrying from my past? Could starting psychotherapy help?

15

What It's Like Now:
I am Happy, Lucky, and Grateful ...

The challenging times I experienced in the past used to make me feel as though I had been dealt a bunch of shitty hands in the card game of Life. I would be angry and full of self-pity, but over time, and with a lot of growth and healing, I am now able to look at all of those shitty hands and see how they now add up to the most winning hand ever. I love my life, today and I love where I am. And more than anything else, I am grateful. Grateful for all of it!

So, if you were to ask me what my life is like now, I would say this: my life is full, and my life is my own. Instead of feeling afraid, I have faith. Instead of wallowing in despair, I am excited about the future. Instead of simmering in loneliness, I delight in being loved. Instead of brewing in anger, I demonstrate compassion and understanding. Instead of struggling with the anguish of pain and discomfort, I am comfortable and at peace. And instead of hiding in darkness, I am bathed in light.

Today I am healthy and well and I am genuinely happy. I continue to seek a better understanding of myself to further untangle the knots of my childhood, and although alcoholism will always be a subtle foe, it no longer owns me. And I am cancer-free. I have taken charge of my life and my health and today I no longer feel the need to mask who I am or how I really feel. My life is no longer a precarious and insecure situation resembling a house of cards. No longer do I live in a world filled with the worry and fear that my demon of alcoholism will rear its head and I will be found out, viewed differently and judged. My life today is built on a solid foundation, which is based in truth and love. My life is filled with love and light and I have been blessed with an amazing husband who lives a life based in the principles of truth and love with me, as we find courage in each other to journey forward.

One beautiful Sunday morning, while I was in the process of writing this book, I unexpectedly ran past what would later that day be the finish area for the Terry Fox Run. Terry Fox was a young athlete whose right leg had to be amputated due to bone cancer and he later became a Canadian cancer activist. His cancer came to claim him when he was only 22 years old and he left behind an enormous legacy of inspired leadership for us all. Terry became a household name in the 1980s. Determined to remain an athlete, he set a goal of running across Canada to raise money for cancer research in what became known as the Marathon of Hope. Today, the annual Terry Fox Run raises money for cancer research in 60 countries around the world.

Because I am a grateful cancer survivor, the Terry Fox Run has a profound meaning for me. To see the banner for the Terry Fox Run while I was on my Sunday morning run touched me deep inside my soul. I immediately stopped and bent forward as emotions welled up and tears poured down my face. Overwhelmed with emotion. I cried. In that moment, I was reminded of the pain of my cancer experience, and although I felt the trauma of the experience pouring out of me, in that exact moment I felt the liberating and exalting release of the freedom I now enjoy. Painful memories flashed through my mind while at the same time I felt completely alive.

Tears of Gratitude

These powerful tears with mixed emotions I have come to call my Tears of Gratitude. These tears are so powerful because I actually feel remnants of the pain and heartache of the past while at the same time I feel the beauty of where and who I am today. The emotions are so powerful that I feel a surge of spiritual connection. You know when you feel so much that you get goosebumps and your whole body feels like it is vibrating? Well, here I am, eight years after my last drink of alcohol, and six years out of my cancer experience and I leisurely run five kilometres on a Sunday morning, feeling healthier and happier than ever. I appreciate my health and feel connected; honestly, it doesn't get better than that.

Tough days still come and go, but today I am equipped to manage life and situations that come before me with courage, strength, and grace. I am equipped as a result of my life experiences and all the tools I have acquired. I like to think of it as filling a tool belt. When you start out in life, you have an empty tool belt. At the end of each experience, challenge or adversity, you can acquire a tool to add to your belt. But here is the catch; you only get the tool if you learn the lesson. Kind of like how Girl Guides earn badges. I think that helps explain why some people in life are much more prepared and equipped than others. Those of us with fewer tools either have not had the opportunity or experiences to gain many tools or we have had the opportunity but did not learn the lesson and therefore did not gain the tool or "the badge." I have come to see that it is much easier to try to look at challenges that I am faced with as more of an opportunity than a tough situation, and I try to see what I can learn from it. That way I might achieve another tool or badge to help me along my journey.

People who know me and who have followed my journey are not surprised to see the unfolding of my life in such a positive direction and with such force. And the reason is that *I do the work*. To use an old cliché, I do my best to "Walk the Talk." The *Big Book* of Alcoholics Anonymous (AA) lays out promises of recovery and we are told they will come true if we work for them. The Promises were written by the co-founders of AA and were published in print in the first edition of the book, *Alcoholics Anonymous*, also referred to as *The Big Book*, in 1939.[21] I think that they are not only amazing but The Promises are attainable for all. Not just for alcoholics, but for every single person who has a desire to change their present situation or improve their quality of life.

---

[21] Alcoholics Anonymous, *The Big Book* —4th Ed., p. 83-84

The Promises

Promise 1: We are going to know a new freedom and a new happiness.

Promise 2: We will not regret the past nor wish to shut the door on it.

Promise 3: We will comprehend the word serenity.

Promise 4: We will know peace.

Promise 5: No matter how far down the scale we have gone, we will see how our experience can benefit others.

Promise 6: The feeling of uselessness and self-pity will disappear.

Promise 7: We will lose interest in selfish things and gain interest in our fellows.

Promise 8: Self-seeking will slip away.

Promise 9: Our whole *attitude* and outlook upon life will change.

Promise 10: Fear of people and economic insecurity will leave us.

Promise 11: We will intuitively know how to handle situations, which used to baffle us.

Promise 12: We will suddenly realize that God is doing for us what we could not do.

The promises have definitely come true for me, and today I live a life-based in gratitude. I have found that I am only able to maintain this baseline if I am spiritually connected. When I am aligned spiritually grace flows in and my experience is that when grace is present, gratitude is right beside it. I have also noticed that if I am connected, aligned, spiritually fit— call it what you like—I am able to experience grace randomly sprinkled throughout my days in moments of spiritual connection that are sometimes so intensely powerful that they must come from the spiritual realm.

I experience this kind of powerful connection when I go to Princess Margaret Hospital (PMH) for my follow up appointments. It's a massive jolt to my soul to be able to walk through those halls standing tall, strong, and healthy, and walk by waiting areas that are painfully familiar to me. As my gaze scans the room, I try not to stare into the faces or eyes of the waiting patients, as I am afraid to feel that fear again. I know the look they wear far too well, and I can almost feel the collective fear radiating through the room. Seeing the waiting area filled with so many people who are sick with cancer, as I once was, reminds me how much I don't want to go there again.

I also experience these flash moments of spiritual connection while attending AA meetings, as well. They usually happen while I listen to someone's story and hear a particular event or detail that resonates deeply because I went through that, too. These moments are profoundly powerful for me, because just as I walked the halls of PMH like many other cancer patients, I have also walked the same path every alcoholic has. I am thankful to be in a remission state with both of my diseases, and no longer do I fear I might not live to see the next day. I have lost my long hair to chemotherapy. I have lost my dignity and pieces of my soul while drinking alcoholically. I have lost people I care for deeply and still love today. To be on the other side of both alcoholism and cancer is a rare and gifted place to be. All of these life experiences have broken me down, changed me, and shaped me into the person that I am today, and I am blessed to be alive and well. To be able to enjoy early morning runs and see my new ponytail bouncing in the shadows on the sidewalk is an incredible miracle. As a result of my intimate personal experiences and brushes with death, I have come to know this precious life is a gift, not a given, This has taught me to live my life with careful concern and for that, I try to not take anything for granted.

I have come to accept my past and I will continue to work on having a deeper level of forgiveness and compassion for others and myself. I have found that the more I am able to forgive and accept, the more I am able to heal. I read in Oprah's Super Soul Sunday book, that forgiveness is giving up the hope that the past could be any different. I smiled and felt comfort when I read that quote. I accept my past and now I can say I like who I am today and I love my life.

I now live in the sweet place of gratitude: I am Happy, Lucky, and Grateful. As I have shared, I take my life seriously, I do not rest on my laurels or take things for granted so I do the work. My LiveWell Recipe is the work required to keep myself in this great state of being Happy, Lucky, and Grateful.

In the next chapter, I share my LiveWell Recipe in hopes that it may resonate with readers, and that it may be useful as we all find our way and our path.

The Question to Ask Yourself:

What would have to change in my life in order to invite it into greater levels of happiness and appreciation?

16

The LiveWell Recipe

My LiveWell Recipe represents a collection of suggestions that have worked for me, and I'm pleased to share them with anyone who is looking for possible action they might take to enhance or support their daily routine. Many people are already successfully implementing their own version of a recipe for living well but if you have not already developed a daily self-care routine, I'm excited for you; building one, and following it, will change your life.

My recipe came to life for me when I was at the lowest of many low points during the end stages of my drinking. During this time I would wake up feeling desperate for change, but I was so overwhelmed with how far down the rabbit hole of misery I had fallen that I wasn't sure if I could do anything. I felt cornered like I had nowhere to turn and I didn't know what to do or where to start.

What I ultimately did was to start repeating this mantra:

"Do what I can—with what I have—where I am today."

"Do what I can—with what I have—where I am today."

"Do what I can—with what I have—where I am today."

I would repeat this until I could get myself moving and then I would dig deep inside myself and do *something*, even if in that moment, all I could manage was to get up out of bed. I realized I had to do absolutely anything to make myself feel better because my life was on the line. On some of those first days, I barely managed to get up, eat something healthy, get outside into the fresh air, and refrain from drinking alcohol.

Like clockwork, I would start the following day with my mantra, "Do what I can—with what I have—where I am today." And then I would take the same action I had taken the previous day: get up, eat something healthy, get outside, and refrain from drinking alcohol ... and then I would add one more action to support my overarching goal of feeling better. By the end of that first week, I had added a few items to my morning ritual and it had turned into a daily checklist. I was starting to feel the benefits, and I had begun to notice that different areas of my body supported each other. I quickly began to notice that my four "bodies"—the mental, the physical, the emotional and the spiritual—were all interconnected and dependent upon one another. I discovered if I did something for my physical body, like yoga, my muscles would feel more flexible, but I would also notice a positive effect on my "mental body"; I would feel calmer and less anxious. Or, if I prayed and meditated, I felt less fear, and if I felt less fear, I had more energy, and if I had more energy, I would exercise, and if I exercised, I would feel better about my appearance, and then I would have greater self-esteem, and then I would ... well, you get the gist of it. Everything affected everything else in a continuous positive feedback loop that pulled me one step at a time out of the misery of despair and towards a life of well being.

Once I became aware of how interconnected these four bodies were, and saw the importance of a holistic approach to my well-being, I made sure that I addressed the needs of each body daily. And, Voilà! All of the actions I engaged in daily to support my sobriety became the ingredients of my ongoing routine. My LiveWell Recipe was born.

Over the years my recipe has evolved. The amount of each ingredient has fluctuated over time, and new ingredients were added in response to my changing needs. What has remained the same is the fact that My LiveWell Recipe is a constant in my life and it has become the framework for my life of recovery. It supports my overall state of wellness and my emotional sobriety. It fosters growth and evolution and, most importantly for an alcoholic like myself, it helps prevents relapse.

I invite you to read below for the ingredients of my personal LiveWell Recipe and consider if there are ideas and insights here on how to build your own recipe for living well, too.

❖ Psychotherapy
❖ Prayer
❖ Self-care
❖ Alcoholics Anonymous (AA)
❖ Removal of Toxins
❖ Effort and Responsibility
❖ Yoga
❖ Truth
❖ Mindfulness/Meditation

Psychotherapy

Pain travels through family lines until someone is ready to heal him or herself. By going through the agony of healing you no longer pass the chalice onto the generations that follow. It is incredibly important and sacred work.
– Unknown

I can't begin to express the importance psychotherapy has played throughout my journey of recovery and in my quest for higher levels of emotional balance and self-actualization. To say that early recovery is challenging is an understatement of epic proportions. It is tough, tough, tough. During my first few months of sobriety, I was committed to self-care, praying, AA and the 12-Step work; I fought desperately hard to stay sober. For the first time in my adult life, I was living, and *feeling* life on life's terms. The problem: I wasn't prepared or equipped to manage all of the intense feelings I was experiencing. I had previously drowned all of my uncomfortable feelings in a sea of alcohol to numb myself; that was how I coped. It was almost excruciating to now live sober and be unable to shift, numb or move away from what I was feeling or thinking.

Now that I was living in an unaltered state, and feeling

absolutely everything, I felt like I was a walking, talking blob of discomfort. It was like having both a restless, irritable, and discontent body and a restless, irritable, and discontent mind. Every fibre of my being desperately needed and wanted to feel different, but I couldn't escape my current state. My mind was in constant torture from thoughts about my life. It was overwhelming to think and feel it all. The first time I quit drinking my sobriety lasted for four months, but the thought of taking a drink and feeling the associated relief eventually won. I relapsed and nearly drank myself to death. My relapse was a stark reminder that alcoholism was bigger than me and I needed to do more to save myself.

It became evident to me that when you remove the alcohol from the alcoholic the discomfort and the problems still exist. You have only removed the coping mechanism. I, therefore, knew I had to:

1. Go to the source of the pain and discomfort

2. Learn new coping mechanisms

In order for me to do this, I realized I needed to add another ingredient to my LiveWell Recipe: psychotherapy. At first, it was a little uncomfortable and awkward to tell a stranger all about my feelings, and thoughts, but I found that I liked how I felt after my sessions with her. I felt empowered, as though I were taking charge of my life in a meaningful way, and this was unlike anything I had ever felt before. In the safe environment therapy provided, my healing process began. I came to realize I played a very large part in my own growth and the unfolding of my life going forward. I quickly learned it was necessary to face tough topics and to also bring forward to my therapist the thoughts, behaviours or information that might give her insights she could use to help me. Even the ones I wanted to hide because they made me feel ashamed or embarrassed. I looked at it as if she were Inspector Gadget and I wanted to give her all the information I could to help her figure out the puzzle of Tina. I knew how integral this work was for my long-term wellness.

I also recognized that it was my "No stone unturned" approach to my wellness that was going to help save me. *I had to keep looking for a higher version of truth.* This is where it became apparent to me that I had to become scrupulous about watching for, managing and sometimes eradicating any addictions that showed up in my life. In my therapy sessions, I found I could honestly share where my addictive behaviours were still showing up. For example, even today, I still slather way too much peanut butter and jam on such a small piece of bread that it is a little embarrassing.

Gratefully I learned to prioritize self-care over self-indulgence and this is what helps me keep even my healthiest addictions in check. I tried to be as courageous and honest as I could during my therapy sessions as I milled through parts of who I was and dove to the source of some of my areas of pain. For the first time in a long time, I really took a look at myself. For so long, I hadn't even been able to look at myself in the mirror, because I didn't like the person I saw looking back at me, and I felt a lot of shame, guilt, and remorse for some of the things I had done and who I had become. For years, I had had a really hard time looking at my childhood for what it was, and with clarity. It was painful to look honestly at both my parents. I easily saw my father as a limited man, but I resisted seeing my mother for the fallible human being she was. I think I wanted to see one of my parents in a good light, and I think I also cut my mom some slack because I shared the disease of alcoholism with her. This may have made me more forgiving of her than she might otherwise have merited, and, really, she was no better a parent than my father.

I also had a lot of trouble acknowledging the gravity of the neglect I had experienced in my childhood. But over time, and as the healthy version of Tina emerged, I began to find acceptance of my upbringing. What came next was my ability to look at both of my parents with compassion. It was comforting to feel this for them, and I feel it for them both today. It was the first step in allowing me to look with clarity at my life and regard the child I had been with compassion and understanding. In time, I began to understand myself better: who I was, and how I had been shaped as a child. I worked hard to learn new healthy ways of coping. It was encouraging for me to realize that I was able to feel emotions and work through thoughts that came up without drinking. And over time and with years of dedication, great effort, and courage, I took my personal evolution to new levels of awareness and wellness.

The toughest thing that I learned about was something called my "Chip." I still remember the day my clinical psychologist brought it to my attention during a session where I was feeling that I was at a bit of an impasse in my progress. She said, "May I be bold?" and after I assented, she said, "You have a chip on your shoulder." I didn't like hearing that, and I was humbled. I still fight that Chip today as I carry it with me in a modified version and I tell you, I can actually physically feel it when it surfaces. My chip holds anger, resentment, and blame. And it also carries with it the myth that I have it worse than other people. This contrasts with the more spiritual truth, which is that whatever our situation is at any point in time, we are in exactly the unique circumstances we need to be in so we can repair what is perceptively broken so we may move towards becoming the best version of ourselves.

Psychotherapy has been an enormous and necessary part of my emotional and psychological healing, growth, and evolution. I like to describe therapy as a way of untangling the knots of our childhood … and who doesn't have a few knots? Bit-by-bit and session-by-session I excavated, in a sense, the warehouse of my mind. It was full of painful memories and past experiences, boxes and boxes of things I preferred to stuff deep down inside me in a place that never saw the light of day.

Going through those boxes was like peeling away the layers of an onion. I feel, had I not started with my psychotherapy and self-study work, I probably would have struggled more with relapse. There is no way I would have managed to stay sober without it. We often turn to maladaptive ways of coping—such as drinking, gambling, shopping, eating, and internet-surfing—to get the temporary relief we need. Psychotherapy helped me learn adaptive ways of coping, which I have built into my LiveWell Recipe. I learned new healthy, and much-needed, ways to manage my feelings. At some point along this journey, I started to embrace the person I was. Psychotherapy is responsible for helping me get to a baseline level of emotional stability, and it is a key ingredient in my LiveWell Recipe that helped empower me to take my life back.

Prayer

When the spiritual malady is overcome, we straighten out mentally and physically.
 – The Big Book of AA

For most of my life, from childhood right up until around the time I got sober, I had never really given any serious thought to the question of whether or not I truly believed in God. I rarely prayed, and when I did it was for the wrong reasons. I believed I was in total charge of my life. Everything came down to my *will*, and I felt that if I just did things a certain way, then everything would go well and I would manage to wrest satisfaction out of my life. I was blazing through life on self-will, trying to manage the outcome by manipulating external variables and situations. We know how well that worked for me.

While growing up I had very little exposure to religion or spirituality. Neither of my parents talked about religion, went to church, or even prayed and, looking back, I realize that neither of them had a spiritual practice of any kind or a connection to a higher power or God of any sort. Prior to joining AA, I only prayed if I were in an emergency and I never thought that it even mattered if God were real or not because I didn't believe S/He was controlling things anyway.

One of my earliest memories of praying dates to the early days of my sobriety when my alcoholism had brought me near death. I was suicidal and in a state of complete and utter desperation, knocked down to my knees, and completely out of options. I wouldn't even call what I did "praying," as I think begging would be a more accurate description. In my desperate state, I was broken open enough to be receptive to the power and practice of prayer, as had been recommended to me by the AA program. I feared for my life and I was terrified that I might pick up a drink again. And so my practice of prayer began, and over the years that practice has evolved. Today I pray every day, viewing it as part of my daily effort to maintain a strong connection with a God of my understanding, and to improve my conscious contact with God. If ever agnostic thoughts creep in, I only have to remind myself of all the miraculous experiences that have happened to me—and in the world around me—so I feel it is almost ludicrous that I still sometimes question His or Her existence.

Today what I do know for sure is I am not in charge and God is the director of my life. I think one of the most powerful statements in the Big Book of Alcoholics Anonymous, is this: "There is no mental defense against that first drink. There is only spiritual defense."[22]

That is quite an alarming statement for an alcoholic. I believe I have no choice but to heed the warning it carries and to trust in the power of prayer because my life depends on it. I will admit that I continue to live with a healthy amount of fear around the fact that if I am not careful, I might drink again. So I also look at praying as an insurance policy against that first drink, I mean, honestly, the chances an alcoholic is going to

---

[22] Alcoholics Anonymous, *The Big Book –4th Ed.*, p.43

drink again are really good, and I'm sure the statistics would bear this out. Let's look at this: first of all, very few alcoholics will even admit they have a problem. Of those that do, a very small percentage will make their way into the AA program. Of those who enter the program, a very small percentage ever achieve sobriety. And, of that number, an even smaller number stay in the program and remain sober for any great length of time.

Some studies show that only 8% of people with addictions actually seek help.[23] Of that 8%, approximately 90% are likely to relapse within four years of treatment.[24] These bleak statistics remind me how important it is for me keep myself spiritually fit, and part of that essential work is prayer. These stats show how incredibly challenging it is to achieve long term sobriety, and that is why I have come to sometimes call an alcoholic who has done so a Green Beret or a Navy Seal of sobriety.

The intent behind my praying is to improve my connection to my higher power and to help keep the channels open to allow grace to flow in. I imagine the channels I speak of are a microscopic network of pathways designated for the flow of spiritual energy. Just as arteries are pathways to the heart, channels are pathways to the soul. Just as exercise and diet help keep arteries free and clear for blood flow, praying and other spiritual works prevent spiritual channels from getting blocked or choked up with fear, anger or doubt. I pray to keep them open and I pray to give thanks for this gift of a sober, cancer-free life. I also give thanks for the gift of my husband, who truly represents for me a match made in heaven. When I am asked if I pray, my answer is, "You betcha!"

---

[23] Talbott Recovery, "General Alcohol Statistics" https://talbottcampus.com/alcoholism-statistics/, accessed November 3, 2019

[24] https://pubs.niaaa.nih.gov/publications/aa06.htm National Institute on Alcohol Abuse and Alcoholism, accessed November 3, 2019

Self-Care

May God protect you from what you can get used to.
– Unknown

The pace of life today is unsustainable, and as we become more and more scheduled and even more stimulated, we need to replenish and recover. The effects of the frenzied and chaotic world we live in can no longer be ignored. and now more than ever it is becoming apparent we need self-care. Let's consider, for argument's sake, that the shortlist of self-care requirements—beyond basic hygiene—include proper rest, a well-balanced diet, regular exercise, and downtime from cell phones/internet. I'd like to invite you to honestly ask yourself if you are allowing yourself adequate amounts of the four items on the shortlist of basic self-care? Many people will answer "no," without question. And the truth is, this is something most people really struggle with, and for a multitude of reasons. It seems that some people don't feel these issues are important. And others may see the importance, but feel they cannot make the time. Then there are those who place some priority on self-care, but their motivation stems from image consciousness more than anything else. And another subset of people feels an underlying current running through them where they don't feel good enough about themselves to even think about self-care in a healthy way.

Self-care needs to be viewed differently in our society. It needs to be prioritized as a part of everyday life, not just as something to be started or taken up when our bodies begin to fail us, or when life gets messy.

I have often observed that many people take better care of their cars than they do of their bodies, even though new cars can be bought, but new bodies cannot. We take our cars to all of their scheduled service appointments, fill them with premium gas, make sure we don't get low on oil, and use them within the limits of their manufacturing specifications. It's time to give at least as much care and attention to our bodies!

Dr. Scheufler's Advice:

Part of the training for my position as a Sexual Assault and Domestic Violence Nurse was to shadow a physician named Dr. Peter Scheufler in his clinic. One day he was speaking with a young patient who had been newly diagnosed with pre-cancerous cells of the cervix. With genuine care and concern, Dr. Scheufler was able to convey to this young girl the fact that our bodies have the amazing capability to repair themselves and regenerate healthy cells, if only we do our part, and engage in self-care.

"Let's say that you are given a car and told that it has to last you 10 years," he said. And he paused.

"Now, think of how well you would take care of that car to make sure it would last," he said. And he paused again.

"Now, let's say that you are given a car and told that it has to last you for 25 years."

Pause.

"Think of how well you would have to take care of that car to make it last."

Pause.

"Now let's say that you are given one car that has to last you your whole life." Pause.

"Think of how well you would have to take care of it so that it would last you your whole life."

Dr. Scheufler's analogy is a good reminder for all of us that our bodies have to last us our whole life long. So service it, be kind to it, use it within its limits, and engage in self-care, and then your body will work with you. Your body is the most incredible machine of all, and it has extreme capabilities to renew and repair itself if only given time and the nutrients it needs. I left my training that day feeling more in charge of my body than ever, and I think that young girl did too! Thank you, Dr. Scheufler!

For the most part, our society is confused about what the drivers for wellness are. Many people really struggle with this. A block for me in the past was that I really didn't feel good enough about myself to even think about self-care in a productive way. Prior to living and becoming well, I was not able to show my body or myself the respect I deserved, and I have to say that the Universe never fails. Once I started giving and showing myself respect, low and behold it was given right back to me. I now know how important it is to honor and respect my body and myself.

Self-care should not be considered selfish, frivolous, or indulgent. The bottom line is that everybody could take better care of him- or herself. I am grateful to have had the reminder from my cancer experience that I cannot take my health for granted. It is such a gift to be healthy and well! I now view Self-Care as Self Love. I love myself, so I take care of myself. It's really is that simple.

There are many things you can do to improve your self-care. Here are some:

1. Learn to listen to your instincts
2. Prioritize sleep
3. Learn to say no
4. Put yourself first
5. Buy yourself flowers
6. Get a facial
7. Start a new hobby
8. Take a "staycation"
9. Enjoy an electronics-free hour.
10. Dine out
11. Sleep in
12. Take an evening walk
13. Turn off all electronics one hour before bed

14. Burn a scented candle
15. Listen to the signals your body gives you
16. Balance your work hours
17. Get a massage
18. Take a yoga class
19. Watch a movie
20. Take a nap
21. Meditate
22. Write a gratitude list
23. Sketch or draw
24. Get a blow-dry
25. Bake a pie or cake

Alcoholics Anonymous (AA)

Difficult roads often lead to beautiful destinations.
  – Unknown

AA helped saved my life.

AA gave me a safe, judgement-free adult environment to learn about my Disease.

AA gave me love and support in a spiritually-energetic environment.

AA helped me realize I was not the only one to feel so broken.

AA gave me hope in the beginning, when I had none.

AA gave me a sense of belonging.

AA guided me to the relationship with my higher power that I have today.

AA taught me a new design for living life.

AA taught me the 12 Steps.

AA gave me lifelong friends and camaraderie.

AA provided a place where I learned I could share my feelings.

AA provides a safe haven for me to go in times of need.

AA provides the opportunity and space for continued personal growth and evolution.

Today, AA still gives me all of these things, and to have this program in my life is a blessing. It is truly an amazing program and I believe it is one of the gifts that come with being an alcoholic in recovery. I always have a safe, supportive environment to go to, either for day-to-day support or for help during times that are especially challenging.

And the amazing thing is that meetings take place every day and all over the world. Recently, while travelling I had been experiencing a lot of triggers and stressors while I was away from home and out of my usual routine. I found myself in Amsterdam when I got to the point where I really needed a reset. Gratefully I was able to locate a noon meeting and as I made my way to the location I realized how frazzled I had become. I was worried I was lost and might not make it, and my stress level was mounting. I was taken aback by the waves of emotion that hit me when I arrived at the correct address and saw the AA symbol of Unity sign in the window. Tears of relief came on immediately. In this program lay my relief. I must say that, overall, the benefits of attending AA meetings still amaze me to this day. Even making the decision to attend a meeting is a deposit in your psyche that leads to wellness, because what you are actually saying by choosing to go is "I want to be okay, and I am taking charge." Once at a meeting, you receive spiritual love and support from the collective energy of the group. It's like putting some gas in your spiritual gas tank and it truly is amazing.

Removal of Toxins

Love yourself enough to set boundaries. Your time and energy are precious. You get to choose how you use it. You teach people how to treat you by deciding what you will and won't accept.
– Anna Taylor

The idea here is to remove toxic people, places and things. When most people think of toxins, they think of preservatives in food or exposure to cancer-causing agents like cigarettes, cleaning products, and UV light. Along with all of these, and many more, toxic people should also come to mind. In my early sobriety, I had the chore of cleaning house in every aspect of my life, both literally and metaphorically. While drinking, I was a living, breathing toxic mess. I poured lethal amounts of alcohol into my body, almost all of my relationships were unhealthy and toxic in nature, my thoughts were often negative and harmful, and I engaged in destructive behaviour by placing myself in dangerous situations and unsafe environments on a regular basis. I think it would be an accurate statement to describe my life as a toxic wasteland. I was definitely being adversely affected and my sobriety and life were on the line. I had no choice but to start making decisions and choices that were supportive of my overall well-being.

Toxic Things

Initially, for me, the toxic things in my life primarily included alcohol, sleeping pills, benzodiazepines, processed food, and negative/toxic thoughts. I set out to eliminate them all, and with all my earnest intentions to stay sober and live well, the removal of most of these things was fairly easy. One of the harder parts, in the beginning, was to keep negative/toxic thoughts under control. I learned our thoughts can turn on us, if we let them. Here's an example: Resentful thoughts I had for somebody. I would run the thought or memory through my mind again and again like a broken record. And although I am not a psychologist, I am aware of how this type of thought cycle affected me and I experienced how engaging in this behaviour could affect or even alter the course of my day. I am a big believer in the idea thoughts and emotions not only carry energy but they also partly shape how our days unfold. It became evident to me it was important to catch myself when my thoughts started to spiral into this negative cycle and I had to learn to shift my thoughts away from the negative/toxic ones and towards thoughts that were more positive. I found mantras worked well for me here because instead of running the negative/toxic thought through my mind, I would repeatedly run the positive mantra. The effect of this shift was powerful, and healthy for me. I still do this today. Because I have to. If I don't, sometimes my negative thoughts will get so carried away, that they can actually ruin a perfectly wonderful day.

Another major concern associated with negative or toxic thoughts is that they have the potential to escalate to the point where they become triggers in the chain of events that lead us back to our *unhealthy behaviour* of choice. Remember the cycle I talked about in a previous chapter?

Trigger → Discomfort → Craving → Unhealthy Behaviour

Another work in progress for me.

Toxic Places

In early sobriety, I purposefully stayed away from places where I used to drink or purchase alcohol. Even being close to them or visualizing them would trigger a craving. This meant changing my usual patterns of travel so I would not have to pass by my usual liquor store or drinking establishments. We don't always recognize how often we are bombarded with things, or how often they are in our face, until we can't have them anymore. Well, I can tell you, if you can no longer drink, it is hard to get away from the social triggers that make you want to drink. Alcohol is completely interwoven into our society and our socialization. Tantalizing, subliminal, suggestive marketing seems to be everywhere. When I first quit drinking, I often passed on social engagements because I was not yet comfortable with watching people drink. For sure it was a gradual process, but over time I have become quite comfortable with being a non-drinker. There is alcohol in my home stored in a cabinet out of sight, and I think nothing of it. For the most part, I am okay, but I will admit, to this day, at eight years sober, I do sometimes get triggered in social situations while others are drinking around me. It can be subtle and insidious, and although I don't usually get to a level where I can taste it, or I am thinking about what I will order to drink the next time the waiter comes around, but I do feel some level of discomfort.

Aside from being aware of this response, and changing my surroundings to accommodate it, it took time for me to become more comfortable. It took time to build resilience and time to learn to live in a world filled with alcohol and yet be comfortable with not drinking.

Toxic People

Okay, so it is one thing to realize that some of the people I had chosen to be in my life were not good for me, but it was another to actually make changes. When I made the choice to live a life of sobriety, I had no idea how the dynamics of so many relationships would change. Sometimes I would look at people who I had known for a long time, and who I thought I knew well, and I would wonder if I had ever known them at all. I suddenly didn't know what to say, how to act, or how to be with them. I can only assume it felt similarly odd for others to be with me as well. When I started telling people I was an alcoholic, I was all over the map with how I felt about this process. Some of the time I felt a sense of calm and I was liberated at finally stepping into my truth. But at the same time, I felt embarrassment and shame, as if I were defective or damaged in some way. At the same time, I was able to see some of the people with whom I was engaging didn't bring out the best in me, and I needed to sever ties with them and create more space in my life. The effort to remove myself from any relationships that were no longer healthy, or aligned with my new way of living, required conscious decisions and actions.

The first people with whom I cut ties were those with whom I had been accustomed to drinking alcoholically. Some of these people were drinking buddies, where the sole purpose of the friendship was to keep each other company and drink. They were for the most part symbiotic relationships. These were the easiest to remove from my life, as I kindly asked my drinking buddies to stop calling me or I used the call block feature on my phone to screen them out. Then there were those who were more than just drinking buddies. My relationships with them did have more depth and meaning, but I still considered them to be toxic in nature because they enabled my drinking. I will admit that, more often than not, this type of relationship was one-sided, as I would mostly call these people when I needed something. That something might be more alcohol or company to help with the lonely world I had created through my excessive drinking. It was wrong of me to do this and treat people this way, but when I was drinking I was self-centred, and really only looking to get my needs met. My apologies to anyone whose time and generosity I may have abuse.

The rest of my relationships included close friends and family members and these were long standing and much more complicated. It became clear to me how tightly alcohol had been woven into almost every aspect of these relationships, and how much these relationships actually triggered my need to drink. Nothing they did was new or different from before, and the disconnect was not their fault. Even more problematic was the fact that these people were still engaging in behaviours that didn't have a place in my life anymore. When I was with them, I would feel affected. And it didn't feel good. I could see the toxicity of some of these relationships created discomfort and it was not good for me.

One of the most difficult and painful aspects of moving away from parts of my life where I no longer felt comfortable was disconnecting myself from some of my family members and some of my close friends. Breaking away from some of these relationships was heartbreaking. In some cases, I felt as if I had no choice, as I felt constantly triggered anytime I was near them. In others, I came to see the relationship was just unhealthy and no longer a fit. I had to face the fact spending time with many of the people who I cared about and loved was no longer aligned with my new way of living.

I never set out to weed so many relationships from my life. It was a slow process and it involved an organic evolution. It required the diligence to be honest and careful about the effect people, places and things had on me, and to recognize how they made me feel. I came to realize that some of these relationships had come to an end. Fortunately, the Universe always provided me with an opportunity to assess each relationship. Situations presented and I would then ask myself if that person was aligned with my new way of living. The fact was that many people no longer were. What helped was to remind myself I had to respect and value myself and really look at what was good and healthy for me. In doing so, I was being true to myself and freeing myself to be open to possibilities. Some say people come into our lives for a reason, a season, or a lifetime. To end or break off some of these relationships was deeply painful. The only reason I was able to make these painful breaks and cut ties was because I knew deep down it was what I needed for long-term wellness and sobriety. There are times when I am sad, and I miss some of the people I have had to let go from my past. But then I remind myself of the reasons I made changes in the first place. I took time—years, in fact—to form new relationships. All of the new relationships I have formed since my sobriety are based on honesty, understanding, healthy compromise, peace, consideration and selfless love. I am careful to not let toxic people, places and things back into my life. I have come to see this process as part of my evolution and I have come to accept me for who I am, where I have been, and who I have lost. I continue to strive to engage in good clean living on all levels to the best of my ability.

Effort and Responsibility

I am not a product of my circumstances. I am a product of my decisions.
   – Stephen R Covey

To stop the downward spiral I was in I had to learn how much of an impact my day-to-day choices had on the unfolding of my life. Everything changed when I hit my rock bottom and realized everything was up to me ... and that I needed to step up and take full responsibility for my life and myself. Sure, some things were not fair, but c'mon, life isn't fair! I had to accept that, and see I had a part in absolutely everything that happened to me. It wasn't just my alcoholism that had brought me to a desperate pass; I had to take responsibility for my involvement in creating all of my problems. Things didn't just happen to me; I actually had a part in the unfolding of all of the events of my life. I was also there as a result of every one of my choices and my behaviours.

I had to take charge of my life and put effort and work into my recovery and examine how I interacted with others in this world. If I were to be painstakingly honest and look back at events that have occurred in my life, there is almost always something I could have done differently that might have altered the course of events or even changed an outcome. It could have been something as simple as changing the tone of my voice, or the nuance in a facial expression. No matter how big or small, I had to realize I had a part in the outcome of everything.

Once the bottom fell out of my life and I made the choice to recover, I could no longer wait and hope that somehow, something or somebody would magically change my life. My old unhealthy way of thinking revolved around the belief that others should be in charge of fixing my problems, not me. When I lived with a self-pity mindset while in "Chip" mode, I felt the world owed me this for all I had been through. I got nowhere until I realized my results in life were all up to me, that I was responsible, that I was accountable. I had to do the work to fix myself. Myself! Another cliché I have come to love is the saying "We are the creators of our own masterpiece." When I first achieved sobriety and began re-building my life, this phrase meant so much to me because it felt so true. Seeing the world from a healthy perspective shifted my way of thinking. It was me that actually changed my life.

I started to see and make small shifts and permanent changes. There was a transformation in the making, and that transformation was I! And it was exciting!

For your consideration: For readers who do not care for yoga, or don't think it's for them, please read on.

Yoga

The purpose of Yoga is to develop the body, discipline the mind and stabilize the emotions to refine us as a whole.
– B.K.S Iyengar

I believe most people are drawn to yoga because they want to heal something—a tight hamstring, a torn rotator cuff, an anxious mind, a drug addiction, some childhood trauma and more... these are all conditions that bring people to yoga. Sometimes it's more basic than that: sometimes people simply want to feel better. This was definitely 100% true for me. I was in my mid-thirties when I started yoga and I was tired of feeling the way I did. I was living in fear, drinking way too much and I knew on some level something had to give. I thought yoga would save me. I clung to this hope for years and I channeled much of my energy towards studying yoga, practicing yoga and teaching yoga. I was wrong to think the practice of yoga would take away my fears and pain and that my alcoholism would magically vanish. I was delusional. I finally came to realize that no matter how hard I tried to heal and become free of my pain through a range of healing modalities, including yoga, I was totally blocked from the sunlight of the spirit by the disease of alcoholism. The only thing that could save me was to put the bottle down.

Once I stopped drinking, everything changed. I continued my yoga practice and continued along with my 12-Step program, and I began to see results. Yoga remained part of my self-care routine, and it proved to be a powerful tool to assist me in accessing, processing, and dealing with my emotions. It was on my yoga mat I first learned to stay with feelings and emotions that came up and to work through them. No longer was I stuffing them down, storing them and moving away from them. While *on* the mat and in a yoga pose, we learn it is okay to feel the different sensations or feelings that come up in our bodies. We realize it is actually safe to feel different things. This positive experience translates to *off* the mat. If in our day-to-day lives we come across a tough situation and are feeling uncomfortable, we can draw on the positive experience we had previously while *on* our yoga mat to help us tolerate feelings that surface. Over time this helps us build resilience. We begin to learn we are stronger than we think we are, and we no longer need to turn to drugs, alcohol, food, or other escapist behaviours when we struggle to manage our feelings during emotionally-difficult times. When we first come to yoga, most of us have a terrible relationship with our bodies, or none at all. Yoga helps us get to know our bodies better and through this process, we also get to know ourselves on a deeper level. Yoga also meets us where we are, so we don't need to worry about having ever done yoga before. It is a practice and a process, not a competition. There is no judgment of capability involved.

I also see yoga as a form of self-care and body maintenance. Yoga is to our bodies what the oilcan is to the Tin Man in the Wizard of Oz. My favorite class to attend is by a teacher named David Bruni. His style is uniquely his own. Along with the head-to-toe oilcan-type treatment that I receive from attending one of David's classes, he also shares his deep knowledge of how the body and mind are closely interrelated and connected. While teaching classes David concisely articulates the importance of learning how to release tension and built-up stress in our bodies by training the mind and body to disengage. It's a form of therapeutic release. Tidbits of wisdom woven throughout each class give students encouragement to take better care of their bodies. After I attend one of David's classes, I always leave feeling as if my relationship with my body has improved. I encourage everyone to give his class a try if you can. He teaches at a studio in west Toronto called Downward Dog. Check it out (https://downwarddog.com/).

Each time I step foot on a yoga mat I am showing my body love and respect through my practice. Our bodies show up for us every single day and, for the most part, we expect them to. I see practicing yoga as a way of saying "thank you" to my body and to tell it that I care about it. Yoga is also a way to ask it to keep showing up for me so that I can continue to be active and healthy. And, of course, along with all of the amazing benefits and gifts I have mentioned so far, there is the spiritual aspect of yoga. I believe this element of yoga is a highly personal and individual experience. I will leave it up to this: the spiritual element of yoga has allowed me to connect with my deepest self. And in doing so, this intimate connection has allowed me to be more receptive and open to everything and everyone around me. This truth reminds me of how valuable the practice of yoga is. Namaste.

Living Truth

We must all face the choice between what is right and what is easy.
    – Albus Dumbledore

Truth for me is everything! I see truth as the most powerful virtue and I believe it to be paramount to wellness. When in doubt, take the truth route. If there is no answer to the problem you're facing, choose truth. In AA, medallions are given to recognize people who have maintained a life of sobriety for one, five, 10, and 20 years. Each time you receive one, you get to choose a word or a phrase that has meaning to you and it is inscribed on the back of your medallion. I chose "Satya" for the back of both my one- and five-year medallions. It is the Sanskrit word for truth, but it also means to emulate the virtue of truth in thought, speach, and action. Daily. I aspire to live truth, express truth and embody truth, and I try to not hide truth in any and all circumstances. I try to live each day with conscientious honesty and truth. I try to not exaggerate anything to prevent any truth twisting and I see lying by omission as an untruth. Therefore I make the effort to inform others of any information they may have a reasonable right to know. Yes I am committed to truth and I feel my sobriety depends on it, but that doesn't make it easy for me to live up to these standards. I get it wrong sometimes, as I share too much, or in the wrong way. Sometimes I step out of my lane and impose my truth onto other people and it can spill into judgment. Sometimes it is much easier to lie a little, or tell a version of the truth, but I have learned that in the long run, this is not a good idea. We all know the old cliché, "The Truth Shall Set You Free." Well, it does.

When it comes to success in long term sobriety and relapse prevention, I see truth as being especially crucial. Throughout my sobriety, it has been truth that has helped prevent me from relapsing when I have found myself off track—or more accurately on a slippery slope that may lead me back to The Drink. Although I know there is debate on the subject, I believe it can be very dangerous for an alcoholic or addict to take any drugs with addictive properties. This includes anti-anxiety medications, sleeping pills, pain pills, etc. The reason this is so dangerous is an addictive substance or behaviour may become a conduit that leads us back to our substance or behaviour of choice. Remember, this disease is cunning, baffling, and powerful. Here's what happened to me; a couple of years into my sobriety I had minor surgery and was prescribed Percocets for pain. I knew they were not required, and I could have managed with plain Tylenol, or, at most, Tylenol #2s. But because these pain pills were prescribed, the Disease in me said it would be okay for me to take them. I should have said something and refused them, but I didn't. After a couple of days of taking them, I thought honestly about it and the truth was I really didn't need anything more than a couple of Tylenol.

It wasn't feeling right because I wasn't being truthful and, in essence, I knowingly took that first step on the slope. So when I got home I took what was left of the Percocet prescription and hesitantly flushed them down the toilet. Now I say "hesitantly" because even though I wanted to do this, and I knew I should, the dialogue going on in my head was holding me back. The Disease in me partnered up with the Percocets and together they were making a case for me to keep them. They were telling me I still might need them, which made flushing the pills really hard to do. As I flushed them, I said out loud to the Disease, "F%$& @#U." If you have any addictive tendencies inside of you, then remember that pain pills or other kinds of prescription medications may have the evil desire to bring them to the fore.

Addictive substances or behaviours buddy up with the Disease in you with the primary goal of leading you down a path of destruction or, as it would be for me, back to The Drink. Don't get me wrong, it is okay for an addict to take prescribed pain medication, but it depends on the answer to this question: are you actually taking them for pain? I have been tested many times in my sobriety over the years, and sometimes I haven't done so well. Today I continue to be tested and "the slippery slope" has cropped up before me on different occasions and in many different ways. I have struggled first-hand with how addictions move around within a person, and I have been living witness to the fact the Disease never leaves us.

The truth is that a part of me—the part of me that loves taking something to feel different—will always like the idea of the relief ensued.

The fact is, any pill I take or any behaviour I choose to engage in that can lead me back to drinking is akin to making a deal with the devil. I have to always remember that even though I'm not drinking, I'm still an alcoholic. The disease of alcoholism lives inside of me and will never leave me. Along with entire abstinence from alcohol, I need to refrain from taking any addictive substances. I will also always have a love affair with pills. I still crave pills, and I still react to pills. Heck, I still want pills. Sometimes when I'm exposed to pills I've used in the past, my response is so strong and visceral I can taste them. I think a part of me will always want them. The Disease in my mind will always chime in suggestively in the background, ready to try to trip me up and lead me to take something. What's saved me in those moments has been rigorous honesty and the path of truth. Truth has the power to keep us safe, keep us on track and protect us from external forces that are against us.

I am grateful today I have the strength and fortitude to live a life based in "Truth" that helps me to say "no" to the Disease that lives in me.

Mindfulness / Meditation

Mindfulness is a way of befriending ourselves and our experience.
— Jon Kabat-Zinn

In today's world, you cannot get away from hearing about the countless benefits of Mindfulness. It seems that everywhere we turn we hear people talking about it, or find someone who is promoting it. With the unsustainable pace of life today, it is not surprising so many of us are searching for ways to better manage our day-to-day stressors. Mindfulness is increasingly prescribed and promoted as an important part of our day-to-day practice to live well. Mindfulness to me is being aware of how I am feeling and how I am affected by my day-to-day choices, my thoughts, and my environment. As I have shared, I have learned how I am impacted by feelings of discomfort and I understand that I need to be mindful and diligent to reduce or eliminate any variables that may lead to discomfort that are in my control. There are many modalities or ways to start being more mindful, and for intent and purposes of this book,

I have chosen to focus on meditation. More than likely, many of you reading this book right now have been encouraged to try meditation for one reason or another. So the million-dollar question is, "What does meditation really do?" And how does it really work? Here's my understanding, based on my own experience of it.

First of all, it's important to note meditation is a personal practice, and, in my opinion, there is no right or wrong way to do it. Even the intent behind it is powerful in its own right. The moment you sit to meditate, the benefits begin to roll in. Even though you might not notice, it can immediately bring your awareness to the present moment and connect you to both yourself and the moment. As you sit in meditation you are pausing and giving your mind time to allow all of your thoughts to arise, and that is why meditation is sometimes uncomfortable. Thoughts continually surface and move through your consciousness. Some float away and some of them remain to be stored somewhere in your psyche. I compare it to cleaning out the inbox on your computer. By taking the time to sit and meditate, and *allow* this process, you are in a sense engaged in the "housekeeping" of your thoughts. This de-clutters your mind, which translates into a less busy, and lighter, mind.

Another benefit of meditation is it allows the recalibration of your nervous system to a less frenetic frequency. My use of the word "frenetic" is based on my own experience of what the effects of stress feel like in my body. Because I've had cancer, I feel it is of the utmost importance to keep my nervous system operating as much as possible in the healthy lower frequencies.

The most common brain wave frequencies are:

Delta—deep sleep   (3 Hz)

Theta—light sleep and meditation   (4-7 Hz)

Alpha—relaxed and awake   (8-12 Hz)

Beta—focused, alert, active, stressed   (13+ Hz)[25]

While we are in meditation, our brain waves move from high or active to low or calm states. These brain wave states are important because they affect our Autonomic Nervous System (ANS). The ANS regulates body processes autonomously and it is divided into two parts:

The sympathetic nervous system (SNS), which many of us know as our fight or flight response.

The parasympathetic nervous system (PNS) which is often referred to as the "rest and digest division" responsible for slowing down body systems.[26]

When we sit and meditate, we lower the frequency of our brain waves, which in turn shifts the ANS to be predominantly in the calming, slowing, parasympathetic mode. Imagine it like this: leaving your body in the sympathetic state is like keeping your foot pressed continuously on the gas pedal and over-revving the engine of your car. Shifting your nervous system into that parasympathetic state is like taking your foot off the gas pedal and allowing your car to be in a calm idle state.[27]

If you sit and meditate for as little as three minutes, you can shift and lower the frequency of your nervous system enough to reap the calming benefits. Sometimes I can actually feel my nervous system dial down to a lower frequency as soon as I sit to meditate, almost like a whole-body exhalation. It's amazing! Therefore, along with controlling anxiety, improved clarity and intuition, improved sleep patterns, improved sense of wellbeing (and much more besides!), I am inclined to believe meditation plays a big part in preventing and

---

[25] Samantha Charles, The Physics Factbook, *Frequency of Brain Waves*, https://hypertextbook.com/facts/2004/SamanthaCharles.shtml, accessed November 24, 3019

[26] Science Daily, Parasympathetic Nervous System, https://www.sciencedaily.com/terms/parasympathetic_nervous_system.htm, accessed November 24, 2019

[27] Project Meditation, Brain Waves in Meditation, https://www.project-meditation.org/wim/brain_waves_in_meditation.html, accessed November 24, 2019

reversing the detrimental impact that long-term stress has on our bodies.[28]

I could go on and on about the myriad benefits of meditation, but I bet every single person reading this right now already has a good reason to begin a regular meditation practice. So that begs the question of why so few of us actually have one. I think the answer to this question is very simple; it is not easy to do. At all! I hope to bring a better understanding of meditation to my readers so that you may be inclined to give the practice of meditation a chance.

But first, let's look specifically at the reasons why people *don't* meditate. Because knowledge is power.

It Is Work

There is no easy way out of this one. One must do the work, and we must do it ourselves. It is one of those things where you get what you give. Personal trainers see this type of challenge all the time; everybody wants to be fit and thin, but nobody wants to go to the gym. Similarly, everybody wants the benefits meditation brings, but nobody wants to take the time to actually do it. In the end, those who do the work, win the game. Be a winner ... Just do it!

The Benefits Are Subtle

I'm sure a lot of people reading this today have spent some time meditating and then walked away feeling as if they had gained nothing; this had been time wasted. For the most part, meditation grants no immediate gratification or tangible rewards. At least when you engage in a fitness routine, the waistband of your jeans becomes looser, or you see a lower number on the scale when you weigh yourself. Meditation provides no similarly visible encouragement when you first begin. Nor do you experience the instant gratification of the physical act of sweating, as one might get in a hot yoga class.

---

[28] Matthew Thorpe, Healthline, 12 Science-Based Benefits of Meditation, https://www.healthline.com/nutrition/12-benefits-of-meditation, Accessed November 24, 2019

It just does not work that way. In meditation, you must wait and trust in the process. You have to have blind faith you will get what they say you're going to get and trust that down the road you will reap the benefits. When I was a new practitioner to meditation I, too, struggled with whether or not it really was all it was cracked up to be. I came across a quote from the book called *The Twelve Steps and Twelve Traditions*, which really helped.

All those who have persisted have found strength not ordinarily their own, say the authors of *Twelve Steps and Twelve Traditions*. "They have found wisdom beyond their usual capability. And they have increasingly found a peace of mind which can stand firm in the face of difficult circumstance."[29]

I wanted more of that in my life, so I kept at it.

It is Uncomfortable

If you are the kind of person who would rather babysit your sister's six kids for an hour than meditate for five minutes, please trust me, it does get better. If it is physically uncomfortable for you to sit still in a cross-legged position, then I suggest you find a position that works for you. Trying different positions, or using props, chairs or pillows, may alleviate any physical discomfort you experience. You might even want to try lying down while meditating. If the discomfort is mental, I am sorry to say we cannot take that away with a prop, as it is part of the growth process. The only way to work through this discomfort is to sit and try again and again. Stay at it. Each time you sit, it gets a little easier. You'll start to build resilience. What we don't realize is, for some of us, this experience of working through discomfort is exactly what we need. The reason is, as we sit, we begin to process the feelings that come up and because we are not running away from them as most often we do, we have no choice but to face them and move through them. The major benefit here is it is healthy to move *through* our feelings and

---

[29] Alcoholics Anonymous, *Twelve Steps and Twelve Traditions*. (New York, NY, Alcoholics Anonymous World Services, 2014) p.104

discomfort instead of *away* from them. The discomfort phase is actually an important part of generating the changes within that will provide the benefits you seek. Hang in there.

It Takes Time

Time is that precious commodity we all wished were more plentiful. There is no doubt it is hard to fit meditation into anybody's morning or evening routine. BUT, the main reason people have difficulty finding the time for meditation is because they do not prioritize it. Meditation is often one of the first things to get chopped off the To-Do list and the last one to be added back onto it. We need to make a commitment to making the practice of meditation a priority. Just as we look at brushing our teeth as a way of supporting and maintaining our oral health, we need to start looking at meditation as an important way to support and maintain our mental health.

It's easy to see why people don't meditate. But here's the kicker: the return on the investment here is something we feel for a lifetime. The return is overall health improvement. Who doesn't want—or in some cases need—improved health? I believe meditation actively nourishes and supports the soul, the mind, the body, the immune system, and the nervous system, all on a very deep level.

Like prayer, the practice of meditation is very personal and all about preference and choice. I have often heard people say prayer is how they talk to God and meditation is honouring and listening to God. I strive to maintain and still struggle at times to have a daily meditation practice. But I keep at it because it is a part of my spiritual regime. I also believe meditation supports the flow of God's energy and grace. When we sit and acknowledge, we are available to receive. In the book, *The Twelve Steps and Twelve Traditions*, there is a line I really like that talks about both prayer and meditation. It says this: "Taken separately, these practices can bring much relief and benefit. But when they are logically related and interwoven, the result is an unshakable foundation for life."[30] I don't know about you, but just reading that sentence makes me say, "Sign me up. Where do I sit?" Who doesn't want an unshakable foundation for life? I sure do.

So, yes, meditation is work, the benefits are intangible, it takes time, and it can be uncomfortable. But if you push through it, in time you will receive the return on your investment, and in this case, it is an improvement in your overall health. Priceless!

---

[30] Alcoholics Anonymous, *Twelve Steps and Twelve Traditions*. (New York, NY, Alcoholics Anonymous World Services, 2014) p.98

17

No Stone Unturned

I held my breath as I checked my pulse—discreetly so my husband wouldn't notice. He was sitting on the couch next to me and I didn't want him to worry about the skipped heartbeat I had noticed earlier that evening. This had been the first symptom I had experienced when the doctors found that I had a tumour on my heart. That horrific chapter in my life had been closed for six years by this point but there I was, checking my pulse for skipped heartbeats. Fear and doubt made me do it. I felt the smoothness of my skin as I applied the right amount of pressure over my pulse point and I waited to register my body's response. Everything was fine: a strong, healthy, regular beat was bounding back to greet me. That one skipped beat had triggered a fear response. I was feeling a little off later that evening, so I shared with my husband the fear I was feeling. In our heart of hearts, we both felt it was probably nothing, but we agreed it would be best for me to go in and get some bloodwork done so we could rule out anything serious and eliminate any worry. In the event the tumour had returned, we'd be able to get ahead of it. There are two values that would indicate leukemia had returned and a tumour was back: a decrease in my red blood cell count and an increase in my platelet count. A Complete Blood Count (CBC) test would cover both. I had a lab requisition for that very test sitting conveniently in my desk, so I headed out early the next morning to the nearest Life Labs clinic. I prayed while I waited for the receptionist to call my number. I prayed while waiting for the technician to come into my cubicle to draw my blood. I sat in a state of fear and felt my whole body vibrating ever so slightly. I swear it was as if every single cell of my being knew what this blood test meant to my fate and to me. In that moment I knew all I could do was take a deep breath and turn the results over to God and the

Universe. I had to shift the gears of my mind back to believing, in having faith in a future

I could not see. What helped me do this on this day, as on every other, was my LiveWell Recipe. It helps me manage everything I encounter on a day-to-day basis and, by the grace of God, when the lab values came back perfect, I felt my whole body relax. I am getting on with Life.

Changing and Authenticity

I love that the person I am continually changes. In a sense, I am unceasingly moving towards the authentic version of Tina, the untarnished version who existed before Life happened. It may always sadden me a little to think of the version of Tina I was when I first quit drinking and started to reclaim my life. I was lost for a very long time and I was worlds away from who I am today. How could I not want to keep changing? The contrast between who I was then and who I am becoming is dramatic, and not just on the outside, but on the inside, as well. I am living proof that if you put effort into your life and earnestly show up for it, it will unfold in a magnificent way. Life has shown me that when we are present and prepared, the Universe supports us. It's amazing. And now, I no longer feel the need to try to control everything. I simply just keep doing my part by showing up for life, ready for whatever is coming next, and I let the rest happen. And happen it does, although it is certainly not always a walk in the park. The not-so-surprising reality for me was that things have not always unfolded as I would have thought they would or should. As I have evolved and changed, the circles, circumstances, and people around me have changed, too. Through these changes, I've had to make some tough decisions around who still fits into my life, in order to stay true to myself. There is an old saying that confirms that people come into our lives for a reason, a season, or a lifetime and although I can embrace that idea, I still can't escape how painful it has been when someone has ebbed out of my life. The funny thing is that every time that has happened, I have realized I was no more a fit for the people I invited out of my life than they were for me, so it really worked out best for all. Although that didn't make "relationship breakups" any easier.

What has helped me through has been the knowledge that setting boundaries to take care of myself, and honour what is good for me, has allowed me to be true to my path and true to myself.

The Importance of Compassion

Compassion has been a key part of my transition and transformation. In my efforts to manage the hurt, anger, and resentment that arose from past experiences, I began to associate compassion with the person I felt had wounded me. I would think of them and then visualize a beautiful red and pink heart and repeatedly say to myself:

"Compassion ... soft, pink, red, squishy heart."

"Compassion ... soft, pink, red, squishy heart."

I would repeat this like a mantra over and over again. And it worked. This practice helped me shift my mind and my feelings to a completely different set of emotions and energy. The shift allowed me to release the hurt, anger, and resentful feelings in which I was swirling. Whenever I did this, I remembered that compassion was the bridge I needed to forgiveness and acceptance. Choosing compassion has served me well as it has been a key component of my evolution to a healthy and good place.

Slippery Slope

At the centre of the addict's misconceived and complicated mind, is the fact most of us feel and think there is some little thing out there that can take away our pain. We fall prey to the idea these things (alcohol, pills, potato chips, sex, drugs, pick one, pick them all) can fix everything. But, what we are actually saying is we don't have faith in the Universe and that we don't feel we have it within ourselves to create a powerful life. But we do. I've been guilty of this type of thinking my whole life and I am guilty of this thinking even now while I write this book. I still fight with the thoughts I can take something to feel better and alleviate any discomfort I am in. Important to note, it is this thinking that is part of the addicts make up that continuously lands us back on the slope back to using. I can totally relate to the slippery slope people like Philip Seymour Hoffman—who I mentioned earlier in this book—was on that led to his tragic overdose and death. I myself have been on that same slope many times throughout my years in sobriety. I can't stress enough how important it is for both the addict and the loved one to have an understanding of what being on the slope means and where this behaviour can lead. If we could bring awareness and real discussion around this aspect of living with addiction, then it would help improve the statistics around relapse. When we think of a slippery slope, we often imagine a toboggan, a fun ride and a safe landing at the bottom of a steep hill. A slippery slope for an addict or alcoholic, though, means the landing at the bottom is not a good one or an exciting one. If we don't take measures to either get off the slope altogether or stop ourselves from sliding further down, we may end up at the bottom, possibly a landing into death.

Dancing with the Devil

Any time an addict steps on the slippery slope of temptation, we are dancing with the devil we call the Disease. I have found the addictive part of me is alive and well, just simmering below the surface, always waiting to take me over again. It feels as though I constantly fight my Disease-related thoughts and behaviours. I just never know when the Disease will come calling on me because it is kind of always doing exactly that. It is there, dormant, and it is waiting. It wasn't until I stopped drinking that I realized prescription pills could have become a problem for me. It is a little frustrating and perplexing at the same time, to know that after many years of living a life of sobriety—while evolving my thinking and my patterns of behaviour, while living the amazing life my LiveWell Recipe makes possible—that I still have to fight urges to drink and drug. I can have no cravings at all for weeks or months ... but if the beast is awakened, the cravings sometimes come right back, quickly and intensely. The lid on the jar of discomfort is opened and I need to feel different again. Wham! It's almost like it smacks me over the head. My mind becomes consumed with feeding the craving and feeling the relief that will ensue. And, right along beside it, my conscience slips back into rationalization mode. Where once again, my body and mind are possessed and ruled by the Disease. I will never forget how quickly this shift happened in me, in response to that first dose of morphine at the onset of my cancer experience after almost two years of sobriety. Just as easily as an ex-smoker picks up right where they left off after only one cigarette, I was pushing that call bell for my nurse to give me another shot of morphine, like a kid in a candy store. The beast made me do it. The interesting fact here is before that first dose in the ER, when I was initially diagnosed with cancer, I had never once taken morphine. My body had no history of ever using it. Yet the effect of it put me right into addict mode.

The point I need to impress upon readers how easily one can slip back into craving again and how many different paths can lead us there. My experience with awakening the beast is it has always involved a newly added addictive substance or behaviour. Once added I always landed back on the slippery slope firmly stuck in crave mode. Craving, slope, sliding, relapse. Craving, slope, sliding, relapse. This is a very dangerous pattern simply because it puts me, or any other addict one step closer to relapse. It is for this reason I need to be monitored and accountable if I am to take any prescription medication with addictive properties. That being said, there are sleeping pills in my home that are available, but certainly not at my disposal. On a good day or week, I can resist them, but not always. When under stress or in emotional pain, I am drawn to the sleeping pills like a magnet. I am not capable of being responsible with them. Hand me a bottle and within a week I will come up with a reason why I need to take one. Whether it's in order to generate a good night's sleep or moderate my stress or the chitter-chatter in my mind, I can defend the need. The Disease gets into my mind and gives me rationalizations to support taking those pills. In these moments, the diseased part of my makeup is deluded into believing these little pills can fix anything.

Because of this truth, I have an agreement with my husband to only take one when necessary and to do so with complete transparency. The story goes like this, recently, for the very first time, I took a sleeping pill without my husband knowing. I broke protocol and in doing so, I knowingly engaged in nefarious relations with my Disease. The next night I did the same thing. And a couple of days later, I did it again. I kept finding reasons to take them. Just like that, the door to the Disease was blown wide open and I was in craving mode. I was on the slippery slope and I was sliding. I was teamed up with my Disease again and we were colluding. Not only was I taking the pills without a legitimate reason, but I also kept this information from my husband. The Disease quickly took me over and began diminishing my reason and logic. At this point, I no longer had any mental defense against this disease and it felt as if I had handed my power over.

When an addict like myself continues to listen to the Disease when it talks, I am actively and knowingly sliding down the slope. Add a little bit of "life is happening" into the equation and I may have been in some real trouble. The dance with the devil of my Disease this time felt different and worse ... because it was. Keeping my husband in the dark about this issue was the first secret I ever kept from him. I felt out of alignment and my emotional balance was shaken. Yes, I was torn. But here was the dilemma: I didn't want to keep the secret from my husband, but in that moment, I wanted to keep taking the little blue pills *more*. My mind was telling me I needed them, and that gave them power over me. My inner dialogue with the Disease was keeping me on the slope, and each night I rationalized it was okay to take another sleeping pill. Every waking hour I kept this secret from my husband allowed me to slowly and gradually slip a little further. The non-diseased part of my thinking, my truth, wanted to tell my husband. But I didn't, I couldn't. Because I knew the moment I told him the truth I would have to give up the pills. My attempts to tell him came up short. All I was able to do was to keep telling him that I was struggling, which was at best a poor attempt at a partial truth. This went on for about 10 days. He was in the dark as to why I was struggling and what might be going on with me, and I knew it. But I couldn't go to him or rely on him for help if I wasn't willing to give up the pills and the secret. So you see, sleeping pills, which seem innocuous— and are usually harmless to most people—became the secret little pills for me. This is the critical point of this story. When this happened to me, I knew I was going to be away from my husband working in another country for six weeks, and in my gut, I knew this wasn't good. That's because I knew deep down that I had to step up and into my truth ... and walk the talk of my LiveWell Recipe. It was me who needed to keep myself safe—and, in fact, save myself at the same time. Six days before I was to leave, I was in a session with my therapist. My "No Stone Unturned" promise to myself, and my conscience, nudged me to share the truth with her. That did it, and I knew what I needed to do to get myself the rest of the way off the slope. Later that evening I told my husband. It was incredible how much relief I felt after telling him the truth and setting the secret free. Once again I was experiencing a living reminder of how light and free it is to live in truth. After all, "You are only as sick as your secrets." For a long time, I had lived without any secrets and to a very high standard of truth. This high standard afforded me a high degree of freedom. For a short time, I was not living in truth, I was really affected by it and it rattled me to be keeping secrets again. The first secret I ever carried was related to keeping quiet about my mother's blackout drinking and the violence that ensued in our home. I still remember the shame I associated with that first secret and how it made me feel. And just like so many people, the number of secrets I carried with me grew as time went on and I wore the burden. I wasn't about to let this happen again. The bottom line is that secrets are an unhealthy psychological weight and they compromise a person's psychological well-being. There is no getting away from the torment of holding onto secrets, as they affect our mental, emotional and, ultimately, our *physical* health. Conversely, the act of releasing secrets is essential to our well-being, and to say that it was freeing when I shared my secret with my husband is an understatement. The point I would like to impress upon my readers is this secret didn't just happen overnight or in one situational moment. It happened as a result of a number of things. It happened because the disconnect I was in gave an opportunity to this insidious disease. There were a number of poor choices I made prior to keeping that one secret and I can walk back through them all and see that if I had chosen differently at any one of the choice points along the way, I could have changed the course of events and prevented myself from reaching the point of taking a sleeping pill in the first place.

Road to Relapse

So I think it is safe to say that it is risky for most addicts to engage in the use of any addictive substance because they represent a "Road to Relapse," not just "One Wrong Turn." Each and every time I danced with the devil and found myself on the slippery slope, it turns out I had been disconnected, cut off from both the God of my understanding and the people around me. When I was able to look with honesty at what was really going on with me during these times, it became apparent I had not been praying, meditating or doing enough of my spiritual work; I was slightly withdrawn and more isolated.

You may have heard people say Addiction is the opposite of Connection. And for me, it is exactly that. The more I connected with my Disease, the more I disconnected from my higher power and my people.

The downward slide in my sobriety always included the slippery slope, an addictive substance or behaviour, and a disconnect. All three of these variables meshed together to land me on the road to relapse.

Here are some examples of times when I have been on the Slippery Slope:

❖ When I needlessly took percocets after minor surgery

❖ When I engaged in a new unhealthy addictive behavior; Bulimia Nervosa

❖ When I took prescription narcotics and sedative medications while sick with cancer

❖ When I broke protocol with sleeping pills

Each time I slipped, I could feel the fear and the effect the disconnect had on me. Each time, I knew I couldn't continue on this way or I would slide too far down the slope and ultimately pick up a drink again. Here's what it's like; imagine, if you will, I am on the slope, taking sleeping pills in secret. The fear is mounting, The disconnect between myself and my higher power is increasing, but I am also feeling increasingly disconnected from those around me. At the same time, I am reconnecting with my Disease, and reclaiming the intimate and previous close nature of that relationship.

The Importance of Spiritual Connection

My experiences confirm what it says in the Big Book: There is no mental defense against that first drink, only a spiritual one. I believe there is something greater than me out there and I believe in its power to do good. When I am spiritually connected and in alignment, I have both the mental strength to make decisions that are best for me and the spiritual sense to do what is right. I have come to believe the mental and the spiritual are closely interconnected and always at play. Life has been teaching me that whenever I am struggling over anything, I am most likely not quite right spiritually. I now see spirituality as a safeguard against making bad decisions and choices in my life.

As a result of my slip with the sleeping pills, I did think about changing my sobriety date. Even though I didn't drink, my behaviours, thinking, and actions were coming from the addictive part of me, and they were the behaviours that would lead me back to the drink. The difference was I took a pill, not a drink. I struggled with determining what the right decision was here; I am committed to my sobriety and I go to great lengths to keep it. The fact is I did not drink. So I decided to keep my sobriety date. Again, my LiveWell Recipe—and in particular the ingredient of truth—was the grace that carried and supported me through this episode. During this time I did ramp up the amount of prayer, meditation and AA meetings I was incorporating into my life to help me regain my spiritual alignment.

When it comes right down to it, my LiveWell Recipe keeps me sober, and in remission. This is supported by my connection to my Higher Power and the cumulative effect of all of my efforts to live and be well. I am in awe of my life at times and I continue to work to embrace change and evolution, always remembering that I am work in progress. No matter where you are on your journey to wellness, I encourage you to build your own LiveWell Recipe. You deserve to enjoy better health and it is in your power to master the factors that will get you there.

18

Mental Sanity—Are You in Check?

We all know people who easily handle difficult situations with a controlled sense of calm, sophistication, and grace. They are often very grounded, even-keeled, "cool-as-a-cucumber"-type people who have a calming energy that everyone loves to be around. What these people have is the ability to manage fluctuations in their emotions with a high level of resilience. This resilience gives them the capacity to manage life as it comes at them—with healthy responses instead of disgruntled reactions and unhealthy patterns of behaviour.

Both types of responses fall on the continuum of what is called "Emotional Sobriety" (ES). Bill Wilson, one of the co-founders of AA first spoke of emotional sobriety in an article he wrote that was published in the January Grapevine in 1958. That "sobriety" word is a tough one for some people to encounter, especially if you don't feel you have an addiction issue, and I invite you to strip out any judgement you may feel about it. It's simply a word that— in this case, at least—relates to emotional resilience and living with temperance. Temperance is not a word we hear very often. The Merriam-Webster Dictionary defines it as "moderation in action, thought, or feeling; restraint," which essentially means the ability to restrain from engaging in any behaviours or activities that do not support us in being our best. It involves being engaged in living a life with balance and moderation. Almost everybody on the planet would benefit from gaining strength in this area.

In my model of the world, ES is a state of being emotionally grounded enough to go through an entire day without getting too ruffled by the behaviour of all of the other humans with whom you interact and engage. Along with that, it also involves the ability to resist falling prey to negative thoughts dragging you down the rabbit hole of misery in the mind. And, on a deeper level, I see ES as having the strength and ability to see all of ourselves in truth and clarity, no blind spots. To be able to look at who and how we really are. And to be able to look at loved ones and others with the same lens, and not personalize it. It didn't take long for me to realize if I maintained a certain level of ES it was a lot easier to stay away from alcohol and refrain from engaging in any other unhealthy behaviours. Emotional sobriety supports our ability to achieve a level of comfort and control within ourselves so we do *not* reach for the potato chips, drinks, drugs, cell phone or any other distraction. And we are much less likely to engage in gambling, shopping, gaming, or other types of addiction. So it's really about our relationship with our best self, and how we navigate our choices to protect ourselves. So, if it feels good to relax on the couch watching Netflix, do you still feel good about yourself and your health if you add in a bag of chips one too many glasses of wine? Probably not. ES is that grounded strength, within, that we draw upon in those moments to resist reaching for things that don't support us to be at our best.

I had never heard of this concept until I attended AA meetings in the early days of my sobriety. And, to be honest, I loved it because it made so much sense to me. Here was another thing I could use to help me feel better and manage better. I loved just knowing it existed. It didn't take long for me to realize the role my emotions played in every aspect of my daily life. Not only did I learn that I needed a baseline state of ES to stay sober, but equally important was the fact I saw its presence at work in my life all the time. I evolved and grew during my first few years of sobriety and I came to see it was ES that gave me the capacity to show more love, patience, and tolerance to those around me. And I will admit, I definitely had room for improvement in this area. In time, I began to see things with a clear, honest, healthy perspective, where the level of ES I was operating in helped me make better decisions and then react appropriately, responding in fairness, compassion, and understanding. I was becoming a better version of myself.

Who wouldn't want to grow into a better version of themselves? ES was key to who I was and how I was showing up in this world. What I was seeing was that I had what the Alcoholics Anonymous calls a "profound alteration in his reaction to life."[31] One, I desperately needed. This dramatic shift in my character was the result of my willingness to do prayer, meditation, and to adhere to my LiveWell Recipe™.

Keeping It!

Okay, so how do we maintain a baseline level of Emotional Sobriety? You may not like the answer. Just like most other worthwhile things in life, you have to do the work. I've learned I have to continually put forth the effort to maintain my ES and make sure I don't become complacent about it. There is no resting on one's laurels in this area because the reality is if we leave life unattended, it doesn't take long for it to start to unravel. That is why it is so important to engage in enough daily self-care to have an everyday baseline level of ES.

In the end, it is really the work we do on ourselves and our day-to-day efforts that supports a life of wellness and the ability to live a fulfilling life

I continue to work hard to be aware, understand, and accept all that I am, and all that is around me, and I encourage all readers to begin to build their own personal LiveWell Recipe for all the greatness it brings. And may you, too, be taken—as I have been— "at the edge of new mysteries, joys and experiences of which he had never even dreamed."[32]

---

[31] Alcoholics Anonymous, *Alcoholics Anonymous: The Big Book,* *4th Edition,* p.567

[32] Alcoholics Anonymous, *Twelve Steps and Twelve Traditions.* (New York, NY, Alcoholics Anonymous World Services, 2014) p.110

Hey, it's Tina here and I'm the book's author.

I hope you have found the book both enjoyable and inspirational. **I have a favour to ask you. Would you consider giving it a rating on Amazon please?** My hope is for this book to reach as many people as possible and one way to help promote my message and establish the book's status is Amazon reviews to speak to my message.

Many thanks in advance,

GLOSSARY

AA – Alcoholics Anonymous is a fellowship of men and women who share their experience, strength and hope with each other so they may solve their common problem and help others to recover from alcoholism.

ANS – Autonomic Nervous System- regulates body processes autonomously and it is divided into two parts: The sympathetic nervous system (SNS), which many of us know as our fight or flight response. The parasympathetic nervous system (PNS) which is often referred to as the "rest and digest division" responsible for slowing down body systems.[31]

Antabuse – According to webmd.com, Antabuse is the brand name of the prescription drug disulfiram, which is used to treat chronic alcoholism. The medicine blocks an enzyme that's involved in metabolizing alcohol. Antabuse causes unpleasant symptoms when even small amounts of alcohol are consumed.

The Book of AA – The Story of How Many Thousands of Men and Women Have Recovered from Alcoholism (generally known as *The Big Book* because of the thickness of the paper used in the first edition) is a 1939 basic text, describing how to recover from alcoholism. It was primarily written by William G. "Bill W." Wilson, one of the founders of Alcoholics Anonymous (AA).

Closed Meeting – These are exclusively for those who admit they are alcoholics and for those who think they may have a drinking problem.

ER – Emergency Room

ES – Emotional Sobriety- A quality of character that is

---

[31] Science Daily, Parasympathetic Nervous System, https://www.sciencedaily.com/terms/parasympathetic_nervous_system.htm, accessed November 24, 2019

displayed by balance and control of the emotions and any subsequent reactions to day-to-day events.

Form 1 – According to https://www.sse.gov.on.ca, Form 1 is referred to as an Application by a Physician for Psychiatric Assessment. Form 1 allows a doctor to hold a person in a psychiatric facility for up to 72 hours in order that they may undergo a psychiatric assessment.

ICU – Intensive Care Unit

Imovane – According to https://www.myvmc.com Imovane (zopiclone) is used for the short-term treatment of insomnia. It can help you fall asleep and reduce the number of times you wake up at night.

Mantra – A word or a phrase that has sacred meaning. When repeated over and over again, it can become a motivating chant.

Open Meeting – Any member of the public can attend an open meeting. You do not have to be an alcoholic, nor have a drinking problem, to attend an open meeting.

PMH – Princess Margaret Hospital

Shakti – A strength, power or energy that exists in all things.

The Twelve and Twelve – *The Twelve Steps and Twelve Traditions* is a book published in 1953 that explains the 24 basic principles of Alcoholics Anonymous and their application. (from Wikipedia)

THP – Trillium Health Partners

REFERENCES

Alcoholics Anonymous: the Big Book —4th Ed.—. 4th ed., Alcoholics Anonymous World Services, Inc. New York City, 2001.

Alcoholics Anonymous: The story of how more than one hundred men have recovered from alcoholism. (2014). New York City, NY: Works Publishing / Alcoholics Anonymous World Services.

Davidson, Peter. "The Truth About Antabuse." *Macleans*, 1 Oct. 1949.

Diana. "Statistics Canada Releases Mental Health Survey Results." *Mindyourmind.ca*, 4 Sept. 2018, https://mindyourmind.ca/blog/statistics-canada-releases-mental-health-survey-results.

Doty, J. R. (2017). *Into the magic shop: A neurosurgeons quest to discover the mysteries of the brain and the secrets of the heart.* New York: Avery, an imprint of Penguin Random House.

"Emotional Sobriety Workshop: Greenwich, CT." *Emotional Sobriety Workshop | Greenwich, CT*, http://www.emotionalsobrietyct.org/.

Fleury, Theo, *Playing with Fire*, HarperCollins Publishers, 2010

Fleury, Theo, and Kirstie McLellan. Day. *Playing with Fire*. Triumph Books, 2011.

Hepola, S. (2016). *Blackout-Remembering the Things I Drank to Forget.* Grand Central.

https://en.wikipedia.org/wiki/Gripe_water

Omudhome, Ogbru. "Health and Medical Information Produced by Doctors." *Antabuse*, https://www.medicinenet.com/script/main/hp.asp.

Silkworth.net. "A Letter From Bill W. on Depression." *A Letter From Bill W. on Depression | Silkworth.net*, http://silkworth.net/pages/aahistory/general/billw_depression.php.

Statistics Pg 95 of book. (spiritualriver.com)

"Temperance (Virtue)." *Wikipedia*, Wikimedia Foundation, 2 Oct. 2019,

https://en.wikipedia.org/wiki/Temperance_(virtue).

Twelve steps and twelve traditions. (2014). New York: Alcoholics Anonymous World Services.

Todd, Carolyn L. "Philip Seymour Hoffman's Longtime Partner Dispels Myths Surrounding His Drug Relapse." *SELF*, SELF, 15 Dec. 2017, https://www.self.com/story/philip-seymour-hoffmans-partner-dispels-a-major-myth-about-drug-relapse.

The Dangers of "White Knuckle" Sobriety. (18, June 28). Retrieved February 18, 2019, from https:/oceanfrontrecovery.com

Wilson, Bill. "The Next Frontier—Emotional Sobriety." *AAGrapevine*, Jan. 1958.

"What Is Emotional Sobriety." *Alta Mira Recovery*, https://www.altamirarecovery.com/.

ABOUT THE AUTHOR

Tina Ruysseveldt is of Tuscarora heritage, a member of the Six Nations of the Grand River, a Mental Health Advocate and the author of *The Courage to be True*, a gripping memoir about her triumphant battles with addictions and cancer. The book details her rise from a neglected childhood in an abusive alcoholic home to a career as a respected Canadian Nursing professional, and it provides a breath-taking tribute to the power of the human spirit.

As a child, Tina swore she would never become an alcoholic like her mother, but as she grew older, she fell prey to the vicious grip of this dreadful disease. After numerous brushes with death, she made a commitment to sobriety, and she created a LiveWell Recipe that helped her regain her mental health, and her physical vitality. Just a few years into her new lease on life, however, she was struck by a deadly form of cancer, which her LiveWell Recipe again helped her to vanquish. Tina's experiences with these two vicious diseases left her determined to put her energy towards helping others find their own way to a life of wellness, and *The Courage to be True*, provides a true and compelling story along with powerful tips on how to do just that.

Tina is a sought after inspirational speaker, an ICU Nurse, a Sexual Assault and Domestic Violence advanced practice Nurse, a volunteer at the Centre for Addiction and Mental Health (CAMH) and the creator of Tina's Recovery Yoga (*"TRY"*), a therapy for anyone who is in search of greater physical and mental wellbeing.

Please feel free to explore and learn more about how to live and be well in today's world. www.tinainspires.com

CPSIA information can be obtained
at www.ICGtesting.com
Printed in the USA
LVHW020327051021
699559LV00010B/63